There are few people better qualified to write about Robert Service than Wallace Lockhart. Over forty years ago, while, to use his own words, drifting around Canada, he discovered and fell in love with Service's work. The discovery that he could claim Service as a Scot fuelled his interest. He has followed Service's trail from birth place to resting place, has broadcast about him in both the Yukon and Scotland, and has devised and presented a musical tribute to Service. In 1990, he, and the musical group of which he is the leader, played a major part in a tribute to Service in the French town where he is buried.

Describing himself as a man of the hills and water's edge, Wallace Lockhart admits to a love of black labradors and the making of music. He has written and produced ten musical presentations based on various aspects of Scottish life.

By the same author:

Fiddles and Folk 1998 (Luath Press)
Highland Balls and Village Halls New Edition 1997 (Luath Press)
The Scottish Wedding Book 2002 (Luath Press)
The Scots and their Oats Fifth Edition 1997 (Birlinn)
The Scots and their Fish 1997 (Birlinn)

On the Trail of
Robert Service

G W LOCKHART

Luath Press Limited

EDINBURGH

www.luath.co.uk

First Edition 1991
Reprinted 1992
Revised 1999
Reprinted 2004

The paper used in this book is acid-free, neutral-sized and recyclable.
It is made from low chlorine pulps produced in a low energy,
low emission manner from sustainable forests.

Printed and bound by
Bell & Bain Ltd., Glasgow

Typeset in 10.5 point Sabon by
S. Fairgrieve, Edinburgh, 0131 658 1763

This book is for John and Liz,
Patsy and John

On The Trail

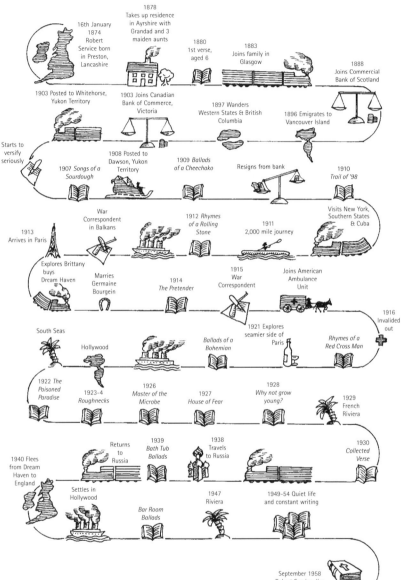

16th January 1874 Robert Service born in Preston, Lancashire

1878 Takes up residence in Ayrshire with Grandad and 3 maiden aunts

1880 1st verse, aged 6

1883 Joins family in Glasgow

1888 Joins Commercial Bank of Scotland

1903 Posted to Whitehorse, Yukon Territory

1903 Joins Canadian Bank of Commerce, Victoria

1897 Wanders Western States & British Columbia

1896 Emigrates to Vancouver Island

Starts to versify seriously

1907 *Songs of a Sourdough*

1908 Posted to Dawson, Yukon Territory

1909 *Ballads of a Cheechako*

Resigns from bank

1910 *Trail of '98*

War Correspondent in Balkans

1912 *Rhymes of a Rolling Stone*

1911 2,000 mile journey

Visits New York, Southern States & Cuba

1913 Arrives in Paris

Explores Brittany buys Dream Haven

Marries Germaine Bourgein

1914 *The Pretender*

1915 War Correspondent

Joins American Ambulance Unit

1916 Invalided out

South Seas

Hollywood

Ballads of a Bohemian

1921 Explores seamier side of Paris

Rhymes of a Red Cross Man

1922 *The Poisoned Paradise*

1923-4 *Roughnecks*

1926 *Master of the Microbe*

1927 *House of Fear*

1928 *Why not grow young?*

1929 French Riviera

1940 Flees from Dream Haven to England

Returns to Russia

1939 *Bath Tub Ballads*

1938 Travels to Russia

1930 *Collected Verse*

Settles in Hollywood

Bar Room Ballads

1947 Riviera

1949-54 Quiet life and constant writing

September 1958 Robert Service dies at his Brittany home

ILLUSTRATION: GEMMA CHAMP

Contents

Foreword

WALLACE LOCKHART'S fascinating book *On the Trail of Robert Service* is an accurate account of my father's life. I think it quite wonderful that although he never met my father, Wallace has been able to analyse his personality so well. Perhaps the answer is that it takes a Scot to know a Scot – and my father remained a Scot all his days – wise and thrifty, and with a never-ending sense of humour. In his work he was a perfectionist.

His love of life never left him. He lived his philosophy, and in his poem *Each Day a Life*, he expresses exactly how he felt:

I count each day a little life,
With birth and death complete;
I cloister it from care and strife
And keep it sane and sweet.
And when the sunset splendours wane,
And ripe for rest I am,
Knowing that I will live again,
Exultantly I die.

Monte Carlo, 1991

I am so happy with the news that there is to be a new edition of *On the Trail of Robert Service* – I have always loved this biography: it is truthful and complete, and the many quotations it includes bring my father's personality to the fore. I must mention, too, how grateful I am to Wallace Lockhart for the work he has done in reviving my father's songs and music.

Monte Carlo, 1998
Iris Service Davies

Introduction

Vancouver rain, Vancouver rain,
Again I heard its soft refrain
Tap – tapping on the window pane.

PLACES HAVE THEIR ASSOCIATIONS – Paris in the spring, London its foggy November, Alberta boasts of its Chinook Winds and Vancouver has its rain. A soggy, wetting rain for which only Vancouverites can have affection.

On that cold wet afternoon in the spring of 1951, as I stood sheltering from the rain in the entrance to a bookshop in Vancouver, I had no affection for that rain. My spirits were not at their highest. With little money in my pocket, I had the afternoon and evening to fill before boarding the train for Edmonton in Alberta. In the early hours of that morning I had waved goodbye to the former ship's purser I had met by chance in Toronto some months earlier. He had boarded a small ship which would take him up the coast to Kitimac where he had obtained a job. Together we had meandered across the States and Canada – although 'meandering' suggests a greater state of leisureliness and opulence than was actually ours. But our ways had to part, and my intention now was to work my way through the prairie provinces back to Quebec, where I would board ship to return to Scotland.

If my choice of shelter was pure chance, my interest in the shop's contents was genuine. Books have ever been my friends, and reading a constant joy. But the stack of books and publicity promoting the works of one Robert Service, which occupied the side window of the shop's entrance, suggested a prominent author whose works were not known to me. Perhaps to remedy my ignorance, but more likely recognising that the inside of the shop offered greater comfort than its dripping canopy, I sought its warmth, and started to explore the contents of the book pile.

And so in simple fashion did a love affair start. As a fish to the fly I devoured the pages of verse: hooked by its rhythm, captivated by its rolling action, entranced by the perceptiveness of its true-to-life yarns. As the hours floated by, my conscience was not aware that I was confusing window shopping and obtaining goods on approval. If the shop assistants were seeking to shame me for overstaying my welcome, I was not aware of it. I just wanted to read and read. My state of solvency would allow no more.

On the night train I tried to recall what I had read. I fell asleep to the metre of lines which seemed to coincide with the rocking of the train. As soon as I had some money, I determined, I would buy one of those wonderful books of verse.

As I asked around in Canada about Service, I discovered his prominence and the fondness for him that existed. Here was a man of whom no scandal was spoken. Certainly, information about him was confined to his life in the Yukon. Little did I guess what more lay in store for me. Suffice to say, when I returned to Scotland I carried with me a desire to study his works further.

Along the shelves in my study there is now a long line of books by Robert William Service. Their tattered bindings, turned-down leaves, unkempt appearance and margin notes indicate that they are friends of long standing and much companionship. Anyone lifting the extreme left-hand copy will see the simple inscription:

To Wallace from Helen with Love, 1952

on the fly leaf. And if prompted to examine the others, they will see the same inscription with dates marking the passing of the years. For the young girl who became my wife was perceptive and sensitive enough to realise that I had fallen under the spell of a writer who had captured my being, and she knew how to provide an unfailingly welcome Christmas present. Thus did my knowledge of Service and his works grow.

As the years passed and I came across the occasional article about him, the printed word was gathered and inserted in a file. I am not certain when I discovered I could claim him as a Scot. But the discovery added fuel to my fire of interest as I sought to increase my knowledge. Not that it was easy. Service was careful to conceal his private life, and if in his autobiography he did not exactly lay false trails, at least he covered his tracks. Publishers, too, can be less than helpful in giving information about their authors. But explorations around Ayrshire brought to my notice a plaque in his honour in Kilwinning. His school was not difficult to trace, but where he lived and worked in British Columbia and where he settled in Brittany were difficult to identify.

The lives of literary figures have always been an interest of mine, and as I approached retirement I thought I might prepare a series of talks about major Scottish writers that I could give to local associations. This would help fill in the time in what I erroneously thought would be less active years. Thus I started with greater seriousness to fill in the blanks in Service's life. Letters by

Wallace Lockhart on the trail – Bow River, Alberta

the score were written, information about him trickled in, and my first talk about him was given to our local Arts Guild. My second was given in Orkney, where to my surprise and delight many were able to quote his verse. But the talks were not enough. I knew that if I was to speak about the man with the authority I so wanted, I had to visit his haunts. So, accompanied by my wife, I set off for the Yukon.

Some places are easy to describe, others elusive. The Yukon is elusive. The 'Silence You Most Could Hear', to use Service's words, is my abiding memory of that land, six times the size of

Scotland but with a population of only twenty-five thousand. Here I discovered that Service lives on. Not because his cabin in Dawson is a tourist shrine or because there is a plaque outside his old bank. He is sewn into the fabric of the place. People would tell me where he used to walk, where particular tales were written. Old papers and documents of his were perused in the library and his old church. I visited the places he wrote about. I walked the 'Merge of Lake Lebarge' and sat in Sam McGee's cabin. I met old-timers and young-timers who could recite his verse by the screed. I journeyed the trail from Skagway to Whitehorse, experienced snowfall on the White Pass and inhaled the very history that seemed to seep out of the timbers of the old 'stern-wheelers', even if they were propped up on dry land. And above all, I felt the vast-ness of the land. Much to my delight a journalist on a local paper was able to give me a lead as to where Service had spent most of his time in British Columbia. Vancouver Island was to be my next stop. The young man in the Chamber of Commerce office in Duncan may not have known much about Service but he knew where to get information. A phone call to local historian Jack Fleetwood brought about a meeting and the start of a friendship. A former forestry superintendent and a mine owner, Jack's main hobby is reading the parliamentary proceedings and objecting in print to everything that galls him. In his delightful company I spent days meandering around Cowachan, 'This is where the store used to be that Service worked in', or 'It was over here that he would sit under a tree reading a dictionary'.

Jack knew people who had spoken to Service, and not all the comments were complimentary, but to visit the farms Service had worked on, to spend time in the beautiful area that is Cowachan, is to realise why he spent so long there. Why Service arranged to go to Cowachan in the first place is something I have never been able to find out for certain, nor have his family been able to help me. It certainly is not traditional cowboy country, and to be a cowboy was his avowed aim on emigrating. I hold the view that he went there to join some friends from Glasgow, and also perhaps from the Island of Islay, who had emigrated there earlier, but the proof is sketchy.

Rue Robert Service, Lancieux, Brittany

One day when rummaging through a pile of newspaper clippings in Glasgow's Mitchell Library, I came across an article by a Canadian, which told how he had quite accidentally come across the name of Robert Service on a gravestone in the small town of Lancieux in Brittany. Events moved quickly from then on. I wrote to the Mayor of Lancieux, who confirmed I was on the right track. I arranged to meet him, and with the greatest kindness he arranged for me to be introduced to a quite special person who (it was all he would say) had played with Service's daughter when they were both young, and whose parents had been friends of the Services. This lady, after making extensive inquiries about the genuineness of my pursuit of Service, then disclosed that Service's daughter knew of my visit, and gave me an address in Monte Carlo where she could be written to. The offer was of course immediately taken up, and with considerable, and in retrospect illogical, nervousness, I awaited the reply.

It is not difficult to understand my feelings. Service in his own time had finished up something like a recluse, and there were indications that his daughter preferred the peace of a backwater. But the letter that came through the post was written in the warmest of terms. We started to correspond regularly and gaps in Service's life were filled in. Eventually we were to meet, and I like to think I am now considered a friend by this warmest and kindliest of people who has given me so much encouragement to continue my work.

When I returned from the Yukon, I brought with me a collection of songs and tunes which originated in the Gold Rush days. Dated and nostalgic, their very descriptiveness cried out for inclusion in my illustrated talk on Service. So, what had started life as a lecture developed into a musical show incorporating not only some of the songs that Service had written, but music associated with the places and prominent incidents in his life.

The musical presentation on Service's life, designed to raise money for charities, was well received. Press cuttings about it were sent to Service's daughter and the people I was now getting to know well in Lancieux.

Service was still well remembered in the little town. To the older people he was remembered as a dapper and polite if rather distant figure, forever walking, or canoeing in the bay. Careful with money, he was nevertheless a considerable benefactor to the town. That, together with the recognition that he was famous as a writer, prompted some of the leading figures in the town and the Pays de Dinan to consider, around the end of 1989, the holding of an event to acknowledge the town's debt to him.

And so the idea of a *Hommage à Robert Service* was born, and it grew from birth to maturity in a remarkably short time. The main drive came from Mlle Marie Dagonne in her capacity as President of the local Tourist Association, and from Monsieur Renée Vilbert, the librarian of Dinan. A former French Ambassador to Canada joined the group, and the Canadian Embassy in Paris expressed interest in supporting the event.

Early in 1990 I received an approach to take part in the *Hommage*, now planned for the July of that year, along with The Quern, the group I was involved with in the musical presentation of Service's life. There was no doubt as to the answer we would give. In a moment of what could only have been madness, we

The Scottish musical group 'Quern' at their musical tribute to
Robert Service in Brittany. The author is on the right of the bard's daughter,
Madame Iris Service Davies.

agreed to perform the show in French, and the mammoth task of
translating the script and a number of poems into French began.
Meetings, phone calls, and letters followed: time was short, the
pace was hectic.

At half past three on the 13th July 1990, the square in front of
the war memorial was filled with the local population and with
French and Canadian dignitaries as the poet's daughter laid a
wreath at the base of the memorial which had largely been paid
for by her father. It was a fitting start to one of the most memorable days the town has ever seen.

The large crowd then moved to the centre of the town where
a large plaque was unveiled to commemorate the memory of
Robert Service. Following the playing of national anthems, in
what was, apart from some family events, the proudest moment of
my life, I went to the microphone to read to the assembly the magnificent final page of Service's autobiography, *Harper of Heaven*.

The *Hommage* was to fill the rest of the day. A *Vin d'honneur* was held, followed by a discourse on Service's standing as a literary figure, led by Professor Michel Renouard of the University of Rennes. A formal dinner took place in the town's newly-opened Centre of Culture and then came the Quern's musical presentation on Service's life. With a little help from friends, our French stayed the course. We finished the day, at the audience's request, playing music and songs from Scotland. My last clear recollection of that night was of what seemed to he hundreds of French men and women performing their own variation of the Gay Gordons. I knew then that I had reached the 'End of the Service Trail'. Nothing associated with the man could, for me, ever approach the emotion of the evening.

A few days later as I sat in the garden of some Lancieux friends talking over the details of the day, two stories came to light that are worth recounting here. Our musical presentation had been a complete sell-out and many had to be turned away. But one man refused to be rejected and insisted he be admitted. His grounds for admission were that he was the undertaker who had carried out Service's final arrangements, and he wished to learn more about the man whose interment had been his responsibility. He was admitted. The other story was concerned with the lady who, hearing of his death, embroidered a cushion with Scottish emblems for his head. Truly, at the end of the trail comes peace, and Robert Service could have made a rhyme about the gesture.

~

The second edition

The last eight years since the first edition of this book was published have seen interest in Robert Service and his works steadily grow. Another biography has arrived on the scene, making, as one Canadian writer commented, the curious statistic that two of the three Service biographies have been published in Scotland. The North Americans, it seems, continue to claim Service as one of their own and are reluctant to acknowledge him as a Scot.

A leading contributor to the Service scene in North America over recent years has been Peter Mitham whom I have come to know well. Peter brought to his studies in the English department at the University of Alberta in Edmonton, an interest in Service fostered during a winter spent in the Yukon. His original interest was in locating musical settings of Service's ballads. This bloomed into a thesis, and after obtaining his master's degree he continued his Service studies pursuing Service's publishing career. Currently he is at work on a bibliography that includes, not just musical settings, but detailed descriptions of the several editions, recordings and adaptions made of Service's work over the past ninety years. It currently features over 800 entries, including multiple editions and issues of Service's books. This bibliography is important because it allows us to measure the extent of Service's popularity, and the varied ways in which others have responded to his work.

In addition to the fine musical arrangements Peter Mitham has made to some of Service's verse, his *Men of the High North* deserves an accolade; mention must also be made of the musical settings written by David Parry and popularised on CD under the title *The Man from Eldorado*. So the verse of Robert Service now expands into the music field. One feels he would have approved.

On a more personal note, the poet's daughter Madame Iris Davies continues to be in my eyes, a very special person. I have returned to Lancieux with the Quern to play a small musical tribute to Robert Service. My Robert Service musical presentation was selected by Dr Colin Coates, Head of the University of Edinburgh's Canadian Studies Centre, to be a focal event when the University held its international Klondike Conference in 1997.

GWL 1999

CHAPTER I

Early Years

Have you ever heard of the Land of Beyond,
That dreams at the gates of the day?
Alluring it lies at the skirts of the skies,
And ever so far away.

The Land of Beyond

ROBERT WILLIAM SERVICE WAS born on the 16th January 1874 at 4, Christian Road, Preston, in Lancashire. He was named Robert after his father, who, with a notable lack of urgency, delayed the registering of the birth for some forty days. Why this bank cashier of Scottish parentage had not been galvanised into making for the Registrar's office sooner is not known. Perhaps he had been celebrating none too wisely. Perhaps, following his marriage to Sarah Emily Parker, a lady apparently of some means, he saw himself as a member of the leisured class and intended living at a casual pace. As we shall see, that comment contains an element of truth.

The name 'Service' stems from the old Norman word *Cervoise*, meaning a landlord or taverner. In the County of Ayrshire where Robert Service was later to write: 'Services were as thick as fleas on a yellow dog,' some of his forebears appropriately kept hostelries, and according to family lore, one of them achieved the distinction of getting drunk in Irvine with Robert Burns. Mining and weaving were other family occupations.

Of the baby's infant years little is known. By 1877 his father had become an insurance agent and the family had moved to Latham Street in Preston. The young Robert gathered brothers and sisters at a speed which showed that his father could be industrious when in the mood. Ultimately there were to be ten children in the family, and no doubt it was to ease the parental load that Robert was sent at an early age to live with his paternal grandfather and three maiden aunts in the Ayrshire town of Kilwinning. There, the elderly Mr. Service was postmaster, and on the site of their house in Main Street, in due course Cunninghame District Council was to erect a plaque which bluntly proclaims how some people in authority wish the poet to be remembered:

This plaque was unveiled on 24th September 1976
by Mrs. Iris Davies, daughter of the celebrated
bard of the Yukon

ROBERT W. SERVICE

born 16th January 1874   died 11th September 1958
whose poems including
The Shooting of Dan McGrew
show a humorous appreciation of the trials of working folk everywhere.

The poet lived here between 1879 and 1883. Later in life he often referred to his happy childhood in Kilwinning. He composed his first poem here on his 6th birthday.

Cunninghame District Council.

Perhaps a more fitting memorial to one who was lovingly, if somewhat whimsically, to write about old age and its problems is the home for the elderly at Robert Service Court.

Kilwinning lies within a very few miles of the Ayrshire coast and the freshness of the sea can be felt within the town. Readers of Sir Walter Scott's *Old Mortality* may remember Kilwinning as one of the few places in Scotland where the ancient sport of the Papingo, the Scottish form of Popinjay, was played. Sir Walter might still have found some romance in the place, but to the six thousand inhabitants in Service's time, it is doubtful if 'romantic' would have been an adjective in regular use to describe the town. The weaving of cotton muslin for the Glasgow and Paisley merchants, on which the town's development had been based, was a contracting industry. The ironworkers and coal miners lived in conditions of extreme poverty. In the long rows of colliery-owned houses, one dry closet would be expected to meet the needs of perhaps six families. At night, the hurry beds, planks mounted on wheels, would be rolled out from under the one big bed in the house to provide sleeping accommodation for the children.

It was a class-conscious town, too, Service recalls, the professional and business people remaining aloof from the trades people, who in turn considered themselves different, if nothing else, from the ironworkers and miners.

The young Robert's friendship with the son of an ironworker was not one his aunts encouraged. Service, though, enjoyed his days in Kilwinning. He could run the full length of the town with his cleek and gird, fish for trout and eels in the Garnock and Lugton Water, and enjoy the festivities of St Winning's day and Bell's day, when stock from the neighbouring farms were brought in to the town for sale.

The ruins of the abbey, the collapse of which had been accelerated by some house builders regarding it as a quarry, provided a perfect playground for hide-and-seek. When something more adventurous was required, the parklands of the gamekeeper-patrolled Eglinton Castle could be penetrated. And of course, being in Ayrshire, there was the legacy of Burns to be absorbed. The moulding influence of the passion for the national bard in that green rolling country must never be underestimated: one must look to the rugby religion in the valleys of South Wales for a parallel impact.

Life in the 1880s was dominated by the Protestant work ethic. His grandfather and aunts worked long hours in the Post Office, and perhaps Service's later aversion to hard work for long periods had its roots in what he saw some had to do in order to make a living.

But if we are to come to grips with Robert Service as a person, there are a number of points from those early formative years which demand our attention. He was brought up in a religious atmosphere, and went through the rigmarole of kirk experiences of young Scots of his time – the Sunday school, the vigorous washing and brushing that preceded attendance at kirk and the dignified march to worship when summary justice was dealt to those unable to control the wishes of limbs to jump and to swing round lamp-posts. In later years, Service would recount to his daughter how Aunt Jenny would entreat him to take longer steps so as not to wear out his Sunday boots. The influence of such an up-bringing can be far-reaching and long-lasting; it frequently stops the drift to waywardness in later life, and one suspects this happened with Service. In the years ahead he was to be heavily involved for a while in Church life, although why he forsook the Presbyterian for the Anglican is not known. After the First World War he declared himself an agnostic, although, finally, he seems to have found a rather individual form of religion. But his memories of these Ayrshire Sundays indicate his pawkiness of humour:

> About ten the bells began to ring, and from the far ends of the long town the worshippers formed into procession. It was a solemn march, everyone dressed in Sunday best, with face grave. Black was the dominant colour, and to show a bit of brightness was to shock convention. As they walked, their slow steps never faltered, while conversation consisted of side whispers: for all knew that behind the lace curtains of every house eyes were on them and tongues waggling.
>
> 'Look! Mrs. McWhinnie's got a new bunnet, an' her man no' ten months pit awa.'
>
> Or: 'Puir auld Jimmie Purdie. His step's gettin' gey feeble. I'm thinkin' whusky's nae sae guid a cure for the rheumatics after a'.'

Although the lad was still so young, there is evidence that already he was developing a passion for literature, and a realisation that it could be a vehicle for the entertainment of others.

The young Robert had a feel for books and a streak for showing off that prompted recitals of poetry and the telling of tales to his cronies. Yet he was able to recount that in those tender years he could enjoy his own company, could dream his own dreams, make solitary explorations through town and heath, and metaphorically paddle his own canoe. We must remember those points about the man in the making if we are to establish our bond with the real Robert Service.

While Robert was enjoying the pleasures of Ayrshire, his parents had moved to Glasgow. Though no doubt the Services wanted their eldest-born to rejoin them, the manner of his going seems to have been peremptory rather than planned. Paying a visit to Kilwinning, Mrs Service discovered her son had licence to roam the streets wearing nothing under his kilt. She did not share her son's enthusiasm for the national dress:

> Imagine how it's braw and clean
> As in the wind it flutters free;
> And so conducive to hygiene
> In its sublime simplicity.
> No fool fly-buttons to adjust,
> Wi shanks and maybe buttocks bare;
> Oh Chiels, just take my word on trust,
> A bonny kilt's the only wear.
> True, I just wear one in my mind,
> Since sent to school by Celtic aunts,
> When girls would flip it up behind,
> Until I begged for lowland pants.
> But now none dare do that to me,
> And so I sing with happy lilt –
> How happier the world would be
> If every male would wear a kilt!

However, such lack of refinement convinced Mrs Service it was high time Robert was brought under her wing, and with some

Robert Service, aged eight, in Glasgow

sadness, at least initially, the future bard found himself in 19 Roselea Terrace, Glasgow, in what was then considered to be the British Empire's second city.

To those familiar with the city, the house in Roselea Terrace now rejoicing under the slightly more stately name of Roxburgh Terrace, needs no description. Glasgow abounds with such houses: a block of flats put together as if by Clyde shipbuilders, strong, open of countenance and enduring. Such places exude an aura of genteel respectability irrespective of their environment.

The Service family occupied the basement of the tenement in addition to the main door flat, but even so, dormitory conditions were his lot, and it seems to have taken him a little while to adjust from being the centre of attraction to being one of a flock.

His school was the old Church Street Primary, and there he remained until 1885, experiencing a good share of the punishment belt, and building a reputation as a fighter. Although reading avidly, and showing talent in writing essays, he eschewed such papers as the *Boy's Own* or novels like *Tom Brown's Schooldays*. They appertained to a society different from his. The character mould was beginning to set.

The new school that Robert was now to enter was considered by many to be the finest in Scotland. Erected for Govan Parish School Board, Hillhead High School was opened on Monday 13th April 1885. The laconic school log-book entry for the day 'School Opened' in itself tells us much about the headmaster, Edward Ellice Macdonald. Here indeed was a man in a hurry, and under his leadership Hillhead was to become one of the institutions which created the legend that Scottish education was the finest in the world. 'He nursed,' says a history of the school, 'his lads and lassies o' parts with all the devotion of a Parish dominie.' The members of the school board took their duties seriously. Within six weeks of the school opening they arrived to examine in religious education and 'hearken the Catechism'. Even so, it seems doubtful if the school as such shaped the young Robert in any significant way.

English was still his subject, and if we are to believe his autobiography, the only one to which he applied himself. The rest of his time in class was a compromise between dreaming and making a nuisance of himself. Authority irked him and the contradiction of being a loner yet enjoying the opportunity of being the centre of attraction still persisted. A sense of humour, which the adult Service certainly had, rarely arrives late in life, so we can assume that the young Service already had it, and this, coupled with an easy ability with words, made him pleasant company.

Just as he later claimed he was not popular at school, so he claimed he was not good at games. Yet, at an early age he was playing full-back for the school fifteen, and his life-long interest in boxing and keeping fit suggests he liked to sell himself short. What he never hid, even at an early age when it might be considered sissy, was his love of books, and while at Hillhead, Saturdays saw him ensconced in some library or other, soaking up stories which nurtured his sense of adventure. Rider Haggard was a favourite author, Ballantyne's *The Young Fur Traders* and *The Dog Crusoe* fired his enthusiasm for Canada as a country in which to live, and Robert Louis Stevenson he grew to admire. Perhaps predictably, he did not take to Sir Walter Scott; he did not like his heroes to be too associated with the aristocracy.

When one considers the countless articles which have been published about Service, it is surprising that so little is known about his parents and brothers and sisters. Although one senses that it was his mother and the younger brother killed in the First World War he was closest to, it was his father who provided the idiosyncrasy. Service Senior was, not to put too fine a point on it, work-shy. When his wife came into an allowance of two hundred pounds a year, he decided to give up work, and devoted himself in his own unconventional way to looking after the family. Substantial as that amount of money might have been at the time, careful financial management was required to make ends meet for a family of ten. But Service Senior rose to the challenge. Food bargains could be obtained in the back alley shops: what if the food was blemished and the fish stank? Like a squirrel hoarding nuts for the winter, Robert's father tucked away every penny that could be saved for the next meal or for the nicotine god he worshipped. For hours he would sit at his cobbler's last adorning the family's shoes with highly individual patches and patterns of nails.

But of all the stories Service tells about his father, the most appealing to readers and disastrous to the family must be the story of the green baize. The father, on one of his bargain-hunting jaunts, bought, in an inspired moment, a length of cloth used for the covering of billiard tables. From this he made suits for his sons. There are times when the reader's imagination runs ahead of the writer's pen, when words are not able to paint a picture because the mind has already framed the startling scene and allocated ridicule. This is one such occasion.

At the age of thirteen Robert spent a long hot summer by the sea, and it fired within him the idea of the merchant navy as a career. It was an ambition that was not to be blessed by his parents, and they frustrated his efforts at every turn. But nevertheless the call of the sea resulted in a watershed being reached in his school career. If his schooling could be brought to an end, perhaps his sea-going career could begin. He was maturing quickly at the time and strengthening physically. The anti-authority streak which so far had remained largely passive now erupted, and like the bud breaking into flower, his rebellious nature, no longer contained by prudence, freely flaunted itself. Now that he could in physical terms look down his nose at some of his teachers he contrived to do so in metaphoric terms. To use a modem phrase, he became hot to handle. Only in English and to a lesser extent Art could teachers command his attention. The end was not far away.

There was on the school staff a janitor and drill instructor by the name of William Walker. Walker belonged to a race of men who are now all but extinct although well within the memory of older readers. Inevitably such men had an army background. In Walker's case this was the Northumberland Fusiliers where he had served as a colour-sergeant. Although on paper low down on the staff pecking order, those drill instructors wielded an informal authority way beyond their status. Loyal to their schools, they took a major part in maintaining discipline. Service and Walker did not get on. One day, playing the humorist and shamming innocence, Service marched his section of school cadets from the playground into the school latrines. His explanation to Walker that he had confused an order to 'Left Tum' with one to turn right was not accepted, and he was reported to the headmaster. Whatever his inner feelings may have been, Edward Ellice Macdonald wisely kept them to himself. But his suggestion to Service that he might like to remove himself from school made sense all round.

Surely the most humorous few pages in the nine books of prose which Service was to write must be the part in *Ploughman of the Moon* where he describes his first job. Having been thwarted in his desire to go to sea, Service entered a shipping office. If we allow our imagination to run freely we can see him as he walks to his new post on that first day of work, immaculate in appearance and visualising in his mind the cargoes he will ship to foreign lands; the tough old sea captains taking their voyage instructions from him; the meetings with Clyde shipbuilders as they compete to supply him with ever more ships for his expanding fleet.

Alas, the shipping office was to be less than that. The so-called ship-owner operated solely on a charter basis and his cash-flow philosophy was to make new debts pay for old. And not only did it appear he had little intention of paying his sole employee the ten pounds a year Service so desperately needed, but he took it as a personal affront when reminded that it was customary to pay wages for services rendered. So the young Robert developed his own commercial acumen. He required two pence a day for coffee and a bath bun to take the place of the proffered glass of water from the faintly pink tumbler his boss used when cleaning his teeth. This money he obtained by keeping the stamp money for two letters a day. Big companies not likely to complain about the receipt of unstamped envelopes were chosen, and, in fairness to all, a rotation system was implemented.

Use was made of the acting ability of the new office boy. When creditors called, Service would open the door of his boss's office, stare inside without apparently seeing the trembling figure on his knees behind the roll-top desk before detachedly advising the caller that unfortunately the master was out.

But such talent for acting was not sufficient to stay the inevitable. Robert arrived at the office one day to find the place empty of desks and hooks. He never discovered what happened to the 'ship owner' who decided to flee the scene.

Imitation, it is said, is the sincerest form of flattery, and when Robert one day intimated to his father the intention of going into banking we can imagine the latter's pride. Perhaps, he thought, he had been more of an example to his offspring than he realised. Alas, Robert's call to banking was based on more practical and mercenary grounds: banks had money and he would be assured of a regular income. Having been bitten once he had no intention of being bitten again. But first he had to appear before a selection board of bankers.

'They were,' he said, 'so sagacious they looked like owls and it thrilled me to think I should one day look like that.' He had, of course, good reason to be impressed by their wisdom. Within a few weeks he was to be employed in the Stobcross branch of the Commercial Bank of Scotland as an apprentice at the respectable salary of twenty pounds a year. Whatever the motives which stirred his interest in banking, let us remember that there might have been one other, and that is an inner desire for respectability. As we shall see, whatever his public displays and utterances, his breaks with convention were not always painless.

At a time when many were toiling for seventy hours a week

Service would arrive for work at nine-thirty in the morning and be making for home at four o'clock. During the day, as an added bonus, there was time to dream, too, and, best of all, messages to be delivered, when he could get into the fresh air, stretch his legs and fantasise to his heart's content.

In *Ploughman of the Moon* Service says it was at this time he started writing verse seriously, and experienced the desire to see in print what he had written. To a boys' paper called *Ching Ching's Own* goes the honour of first publishing his verse, although more mature if somewhat romantic publications like the *People's Friend* were not to be so far behind. The *Glasgow Herald* also recognised his youthful talent as a versifier.

Service was by now experiencing the first pangs of calf love, but found the writing of verse more stirring to the heart and of greater appeal than the harder work and expense of conventional forms of courtship. Much of his verse pleased him: one sonnet of love he claimed, 'was so good I was able to use it with three different girls.' Modestly, he declines to say with what success.

Still an avid reader, Service carried books to the bank, for reading when the accountant's eye was not focused on him. The habit he also carried into the streets, reading in a way which might he called detrimental to public safety, as with eyes on his book he crossed roads carrying their fleets of solid-tyred bicycles and horse-drawn trams.

Browning and Tennyson he claimed as his special favourites. Thackeray and Keats also had his allegiance. But as he matured there was one form of entertainment which would for a while first overtake and then swamp his enthusiasm for poetry.

Perhaps too early in life, Service discovered the music hall. Not that the music hall reduced his interest in simple verse: it may have stimulated it. But from now on whenever he settled down with pen and paper to write, the ugly would be just as important as the beautiful, the tangible as vital as the abstract, vice more attractive than virtue, and the talk of the man in the street would eclipse the protestations of the poet in my lady's bower.

You see, a common bloke am I
And vulgar ways I go;
I sit in pubs and on the sly
Enjoy a good leg show.
So if you be with culture crammed
You'll scorn the likes o' me
Hell! What of it? If I be damned
I've lots of company.

Without conscious decision Service was now on the road to writing verses for the masses, or, as he would so graphically describe it later, 'writing verse for those who wouldn't be seen dead reading poetry'.

In a city which could boast of a history of buildings created specifically for theatrical purposes going back to 1752, it was not surprising that young men like Service, smitten by the rowdy, beery, pie-smelling environment of the music halls could find plenty of places where their lungs could be exercised. G.J. Mellor in his *Northern Music Halls* gives an intimate account of what Glasgow had to offer in Service's time.

> But Glasgow was really the place for the old-time music hall in Scotland. The residents of the 'St Mungo' city are really pleasure-conscious, now as then, and it is not surprising that there were many places of amusement ready and willing to cater for the Glaswegians' pleasure.
>
> The Scotia opened in 1862 and at that time there was Davy Brown's Philharmonic (or Follys) in Dunlop Street, Shearer's Whitebait in St Enoch's Wynd, Sloan's Oddfellows in Argyle St.; 'Free and Easies' called the Jupiter and the Shakespeare in the Saltmarket, and two places run by Willie Campbell (champion sculler in the West of Scotland) – Levy's at the Glasgow Cross and a place in the Trongate, known as Campbell's.
>
> The Whitebait was a very curious house, with the performers 'wired in', so that the audience, (usually boisterous) could not jump on the stage and dance with them.

The Free and Easies like the Jupiter and Shakespeare were licensed singing saloons containing a small stage and a piano where amateurs were encouraged to provide most of the entertainment. Admission was usually free, although some, seeking to be up-market, would charge a shilling, softening the blow by presenting the customer with a cigar. The proceedings were conducted by a Chairman, who, remembering that the objective of licensed premises is to sell beer, would encourage the clientele to a thirst by coercing them to sing, as lustily as possible, the popular choruses of the day.

To many of Service's friends, the regular round of music hall evenings would be an end in themselves; work and play were two parts of life to be lived out separately. But to Service the happiness given to him by the music hall was to stir thoughts of a career for himself on the stage. Not, of course, on the uncouth boards of the music hall, but the more socially acceptable legitimate stage.

Once again we see this shaft of longing for respectability forcing its way through. The metamorphosis was not to be abrupt. Appearances being important, he first had to look like an actor, to behave like an actor. Theatrical newspapers had to be studied in an affected way as he sat on the top of a tram. The jargon had to be learned, and the company of those on the fringe of theatrical success cultivated.

He started elocution lessons and returned to poetry; not the reading of it for self-enjoyment but the learning of it so that he could give recitations which would lead to basking in the plaudits of audiences recognising what he felt sure were his many and great talents. Like all adolescents, Service was a dreamer.

And progress was made, for Service always had energy for those pursuits which were of interest to him. Church-hall concerts were his first venues, followed by apprenticeship walk-on parts in the real theatre.

Then came the break-through, the opportunity to place his foot on the first rung of the ladder to stardom. He was asked to play the son of the named hero in an amateur production of *Rob*

Roy. The lines were not onerous to learn. On cue, his part was to rush on stage and explain to the ample-bosomed lady playing his mother that Rob Roy had been captured. On receiving this sad news the noble lady would hug him tight and share her grief with her son.

Unfortunately, come the night, the prospect of fame had gone to the young actor's head, and having put on the necessary Highland garb for the part, he accepted a colleague's invitation to have a drink in a bar adjoining the theatre – a not uncommon practice, it has to be said. It was while knocking back more than his first that another actor arrived to tell him that his stage mother, a staunch teetotaller, had vowed to spank him for daring to drink before acting. Jokingly his friend swung his sporran round to the rear. 'That'll give you protection,' he said, as the call-boy shouted from the bar doorway to Service that he was on. Service put down his glass and raced for the stage. Half-hearing the stage-manager's cry that he had his kilt on back to front, he tripped into the arms of his stage mother, who, incensed by the fumes of alcohol being breathed into her face, venomously spurned his efforts to console her on the loss of her husband. The scene ended in chaos as Service prematurely left the stage. It was to be some years before the footlights would see him again.

Our pursuit of Service now takes us to the University of Glasgow. Like countless others he had felt the peculiar pull of those academic enclaves which stand on a hill, so apart from the city, and yet so much part of it. No discouraging remarks about the university are to be heard in Glasgow from even the most unlikely of prospective entrants. The University, like the Burrell Collection and other havens of culture, has the Glaswegians' allegiance, whether or not the portals are ever crossed.

But something at this time drew Service to the formal study of literature, and having paid his two guinea fee for the year, he started his classes. For an hour a day, outwith bank hours, he would undertake, according to the prospectus of the time, such challenges as the growth of the English language and its affinities with other tongues, the general principles of taste and style and the criticism of some works of the more difficult authors. There were, he recounts, about two hundred in the class, and nearly all, he thought, deserved his sympathy. 'They were,' he said, 'poor boobs to be pitied.'

Destined in the main for the manse, they lacked his ability, he was sure, to drink bitter beer and chat up barmaids. Yet he did well in his studies, coming fourth in the Christmas examination, and he must be displaying modesty when he puts his success down to learning the Professor's notes off by heart. But in the second term he started to become unstuck. The pressure to conform to academic views of literature began to niggle. He wanted his own interpretations to be recognised.

In an essay on Ophelia he suggested that she was less than pure, and that this was the cause of Hamlet's distracted condition. The lecturer's written comment on the exam paper that it was a 'perverse and obscene bit of work – unworthy of a student of this class' stung him to retribution. A challenge to fisticuffs was made but not accepted by the lecturer. Disenchanted, Service left the University. Another experience was over.

Yet, just as he was to retain affection for his old school, so would he retain affection for Glasgow University. Always with Service we must look for deeds rather than accept his words whole-heartedly. The University Court Minute 165 of 21st December 1961 makes telling reading:

> It was reported that Madame Service, of Monte Carlo, widow of the Scottish Canadian poet Robert Service, had offered to endow an annual prize in the Ordinary class of English in memory of her husband. To this end she had already placed to the credit of her Glasgow agent, Mr Arthur H. Stewart of Skerry's College, the sum of $3000.

Perhaps he didn't tell Madame Service about his affair with Ophelia – perhaps he just mentioned the fourth prize.

Service's studies had taken up a good deal of his spare time and inevitably the ending of them caused a vacuum in his life. As he would so often do when unsettled, he immersed himself in the books of writers whose life style he was in so many ways to emulate, such as Stevenson the restless bohemian, and Kipling, whose life under the Raj was to point him to the barrack room rather than to the officers' mess for colour.

Yet books were not enough. Youths, especially dreamy youths need passionate outlets, and Service was now to find a cause he could proclaim and debate. A small book by the name of *Merrie England* converted him overnight into a socialist. With an enthusiasm akin to a Road to Damascus conversion he preached against the iniquities of social injustice, reviled the rich, and bored his friends to tears.

Avidly he read political pamphlets and attended meetings, fired with his new-found calling in life to make the world a better place:

It's my belief that every man
Should do his share of work,
And in our economic plan
No citizen should shirk.
That in return each one should get
His meed of fold and food,
And feel that all his toil and sweat
Is for the common good.
It's my belief that people should
Be neither rich nor poor;
That none should suffer servitude,
And all should be secure.
That wealth is loot, and rank is rot,
And foul is class and clan;
That to succeed a man may not
Exploit his brother man.

And then this world, too, began to crumble. The socialists, he found, were not too keen on this well dressed, securely-employed young man, defending their cause.

When young I was a Socialist
Despite my tender years;

No blessed chance I ever missed
To slam the profiteers.
Yet though a fanatic I was,
And cursed aristocrats,
The party chucked me out because
I sported spats.

The working man, he discovered, was more excited by football than politics. The active socialists began to irritate him because of their restricted vision and constant moaning about the class structure. It was a case of 'Socialism – Yes: Socialists – No', and with a sigh of relief his friends welcomed him back into their company.

Not so much a loner at that time as he was to become in later years, Service as a youth obviously enjoyed the companionship of a large circle of friends. And there was a similarity about them; quite a number were to make their name in journalism. The company of girls was largely eschewed, and he recounted that sport and the theatre and stories about work were their main topics of conversation.

Amongst his peers, Service's ability to make amusing rhymes was welcomed, yet his introduction of French writers like Hugo and Balzac into the conversation was in no way considered incongruous.

And so we build up a picture of Service in his late teens, a clean, physically fit young man, not over-impressed by work, well-read and articulate and inclined to the simple and ordinary things in life for his pleasure.

Yet within him was a conflict; the desire for a safe respectable existence warred with a spirit that was restless, that needed new experiences and movement. This was the spirit that was now coming to the fore. More and more his reading was about men who had taken their destinies into their own hands and crossed the seas to seek fame, fortune or just their own true selves.

And now two happenings in combination were to shape his future. First, a younger brother who had left home a rather frail specimen to work on a farm in Fife returned home on holiday in superb physical condition and impressed Service with the pride he displayed in the work he was doing. This sharpened his urge to lead a more active outdoor life. Second, although he had read all the emigration pamphlets and could visualise himself in Canada, the most Scottish of all the colonial environments, he did not possess the necessary money to get there. That was now to change as the bank transferred him from Stobcross to a city branch at a salary of £70 a year, a gigantic increase. So, now his course was set. He decided to save hard, get himself up to the peak of physical condition, and make for Canada where he would savour the life of the cowboy.

The expressions of incredulity from his family and friends when he told them of his intentions merely strengthened his resolve to see things through. Then came the day when, his arrangements made, he entered the bank manager's office to tender his resignation.

With some nervousness he explained to the august figure what it was he wanted to do with his life. The sermon from the manager on the stupidity of his actions, and the question 'You know if you serve another forty years you may retire on a pension?' left him, he was to admit, short of reply. And then, as Service stood in silence, the manager's face, he recalled, softened in feature. 'I only wish I had your years, lad,' he said, 'then, by God, I'd go along with you.'

> In the April of 1948 the editor of *The Griffin*, the staff magazine of the Commercial Bank of Scotland, interviewed a holidaying Robert Service and asked if he had any advice for young bankers. The response warrants framing. 'Don't try to write poetry and tote columns of figures at the same time – and give every customer the same glad smile you would give a glamorous blonde.'

CHAPTER 2

Wandering Years

Because my life was drab and stale
In stifled city air
With careless heart I took the trail
That led to anywhere

The Trail of Trouble

WITH HIS DECLARED INTEREST in becoming a cowboy, it might
have been expected that Service would head for Southern Alberta
or the Cariboo Country of British Columbia. Instead, he elected to
make for the Cowichan Valley on Vancouver Island where the
term 'prairie' was used to describe scrub land, and a ranch was a
farm of modest size. In 1896 British Columbia was still a remote
colony. The transcontinental railroad which enticed it into
Confederation had only been completed eleven years earlier when
Lord Strathcona drove the last spike in the Eagle Pass in the
Rockies. The building of the Canadian Pacific Railway had so
drained the country's resources that a completely undecorated
spike was used for the ceremony. (This was probably just as well,
as the former Hudson's Bay Company man from Labrador bent
the first spike given to him so badly that it had to be replaced.)

Service never chose to explain why he made for the Cowichan
Valley. However it is known that he later stayed with a family by
the name of Mutter, at Somenos in the valley. James Mutter hailed
originally from Islay, where his family owned a distillery, and in
1889 he moved to Glasgow with his wife and six children, and
later sailed to Canada. It is possible Service knew the family in
Glasgow, and like many other aspiring emigrants decided to make
for a place where he had a contact.

It was certainly an unusual place to make for: there are records of trading with the Cowichan band of Indians in the 1850s, but there was no white settlement in the Valley at that time. On August 15th 1862, *The Colonial*, the newspaper of the growing town of Victoria, carried the official announcement that H.M.S. Hecate would make a special journey to land prospective settlers at Cowichan. How many budding frontiersmen and women made the journey is not known, but by 1866 the Episcopal church which they built could boast a congregation of thirty-six.

Amongst his good-byes, Service included a trip to Kilwinning to see his maiden aunts, but 'with the cruel egoism of youth,' he wrote, 'I seldom thought of the life I had left behind. I rarely remembered my friends and they grew more vague as time went on.' Others were to agree with this comment over the years.

Service enjoyed the journey to Vancouver Island. He carried with him a copy of Stevenson's *The Amateur Emigrant*, but, disdaining Stevenson's desire for privacy, he travelled steerage. One of the first lessons Service learned as his train puffed its way across Canada was that expenditure without income leads quickly to poverty, and his westward travel was accompanied by a steady sale of his goods and chattels to provide money for food.

Journey's end meant a necessary and swift introduction to the hard physical toil he was seldom to escape over the next few years. In his autobiography, Service seeks to conceal the identity of many of the people he lived and worked with, and his Cowichan Valley acquaintances, particularly, come into this category. His first employers, he claims, were the MacTartans from Shetland, which is as unlikely a combination of name and origin as can be imagined. There was, though, a Shetland family by the name of Colvin at MacPhersons Landing. Mrs Colvin was an expert spinner and knitter and has gone down in history as the person who taught the Fair Isle pattern to the local Indian women. Today, Indian-made Cowichan sweaters with the pattern form one of the most distinctive exports of the valley.

Most of the people at Cowichan were of English or Scottish stock and intensely proud of their old school ties. Sport of all

The little church at Cowichan on Vancouver Island where
Robert Service sang in the choir and took part in amateur dramatics

kinds dominated their existence, and they still regarded themselves
as British Columbians rather than Canadians. Many carried the
tag of Remittance Man, the name given to the member of the family sent out from the 'old country' because he was considered a
black sheep, or perhaps because the home business or estate could
not support him. And while the physical conditions were frontier,
Victorian-age values had to be maintained; gentility was wedded
to hard physical labour, of that there was no choice. Those who
did not work went under, but such cases were very hard to find.

Service spent some six months with the Shetland couple, enjoying the company especially of their two sons. He then moved to a
more remote ranch, where, in the company of a rugged old-timer
called Hank he spent a pleasant year working, learning to play the
banjo and digesting, he recalls, a huge pile of old magazines. Here,
too, he started to entertain his local acquaintances with songs and
recitations. But satisfying as this year seems to have been to him, he
was aware it was a transitory period. He felt spasms of desire to be
a writer, but more strongly he felt the need to stretch his legs and see
more country.

Leaving Hank, Service took up employment with George Treffry Corfield, an expansionist-minded Cornishman, who eventually was to farm almost all the land around Cowichan Bay. Service's job was to look after the cows, and frequently his working day would stretch to sixteen hours. With little suggestion of regret, he wrote that 'there was nothing Don Juanish about us farm hands. When a man works sixteen hours a day, it takes all the lasciviousness out of his system.'

But his basic dislike of monotonous work was again to surface, and towards the end of 1897 the open road was calling ever more strongly. He decided to make for warmer climes. He had established a good relationship with Corfield and felt a sense of security with him: their paths were to cross again. By now he was aware he had joined that body of men who were forever restless – the men who don't fit in:

> There's a race of men that don't fit in,
> A race that can't stay still;
> So they break the hearts of kith and kin,
> And they roam the world at will.
> They range the field and they rove the flood,
> And they climb the mountain's crest;
> Theirs is the curse of the gypsy blood,
> And they don't know how to rest.
>
> If they went straight they might go far;
> They are strong and brave and true;
> But they're always tired of the things that are,
> And they want the strange and new.
> They say: 'Could I find my proper groove
> What a deep mark I would make!'
> So they chop and change, and each fresh move
> Is only a fresh mistake.

Even today the short sea journey from Victoria to Seattle has an excitement to it, travelling from one of the most British of cities to one of the most obviously American. In Service's time the difference must have been more marked, although in other ways. The movement then was from a sedate colonial outpost, not yet showing signs of size or expansion, to the bustling whaling port filled with the ships of all nations, and with its warrens of waterside bars better avoided by those who sought a safe and cosy bed at nights. Even into the 1890s the shanghaiing of seamen was not an uncommon occurrence.

But Seattle was no long-term resting place for Service. Like his hero Stevenson before him, he could not resist the Mecca-like pull of California. Soon, as he sat in the Plaza in San Francisco, looking at the memorial to the great story-teller, which had been unveiled only a month earlier, he experienced that unusual peace which can come to a traveller when he encounters a link with home. 'In this quiet square,' he wrote, 'amid the fever and tumult, I dreamed by the hour and seemed to find my soul again.'

A Robert Service in line with the public's perception of the man

Yet it was the vice of the Barbary Coast which fascinated him. Too fearful and too wise to enter, he found excitement at being in the proximity of opium dens and brothels, and, from the vantage point of a window seat, the sleaziness of the tap rooms with their underworld characters provided him with theatrical entertainment. It seems reasonable to suggest that, after proving to himself that he could live through the depravity of places like the Barbary Coast, and could look after himself physically when the occasion demanded, he would from now on have enough confidence in himself to go anywhere, mix in any company and tackle anything that came his way.

Certainly the next two years were to suggest this was so. This was Service's aimless, wandering period when, without insult, we may term him a drifter as he meandered and covered the miles as far south as Mexico, frequently walking barefoot to save shoe leather. For work he accepted anything – the gruelling pick and shovel labour on a tunnelling scheme, dish-washer, orange picker, sandwichboard man (an ideal job, he thought, for a poet) and in the environs of a house of dubious repute he spent a contented and moral few weeks as a gardener and handyman. He was still averse to hard work; his preference for half the wage and half the work continued, and he developed to a fine art the techniques of living on the most meagre supply of money.

He was later to write:

> If my boyish ambition was to be a sailor, my youthful one was to be a hobo. Queer that! A lad brought up in sanctimonious Scotland aspiring to be an American bum. To starve and suffer cold, to beat my way on trains, to live adventure, to emerge with a wealth of rueful experience... I see now I was crazy for freedom, for colour; and besides, I had a predilection for the disreputable. In any case, I went.

> I never became a hard-boiled hobo. I only indulged in spells of vagrancy, and between them I either worked or lived on the money I had made. I had a horror of going broke, and at the worst I kept ten cents between myself and the wolf.

In Los Angeles he managed to subsist for nine weeks on a dollar a week. And the city had a stimulating effect on him. 'San

Francisco made me want to write stories', he was later to say, 'but Los Angeles made me want to make poetry'. This he did, getting a few lines accepted by a local paper, although he was not paid for it. He rose late, he recalled, and ate three doughnuts slowly, trying to imagine they were six. At lunch time, he would elect to sit at a cafe table where the diners had not finished all their bread, so providing himself with an extra course. Siesta would be followed by a visit to the fruit market to pick up items falling off the delivery wagons, and many an old soldier would admire his eye for the main chance and the progress he made at the nightly Pacific Gospel Saloon. From the ranks of those whose praying was rewarded with a supper, he stepped forward to volunteer for dishwashing duties. This brought him physical if not spiritual crumbs of comfort, and his honest face and mild manners encouraged the gospel leader to entrust him with the job of cutting and spreading the bread, a job which allowed him to fill his stomach, although it perhaps did nothing for his soul. And in this town where the Spanish atmosphere lingered and the story of the early Franciscan Fathers who called their mission Pueblo de la Reina de los Angelos had still not been erased from memory, there was also food for his mind. He made much use of the Public Library and had the satisfaction of seeing his name in print again as a newspaper published some of his verse.

If Service was allergic to hard work there was one form of exercise he never shied away from and that was walking. He could accomplish thirty miles a day with ease. Pleasure in his own company meant that he enjoyed the nights when he slept on the beaches under the stars listening to the giant Pacific rollers crashing on to the shore. With less enjoyment, we assume, he stretched out in the rattlesnake-inhabited country of the South and West as he followed the open trail.

Service was a keen musician. He played many instruments, and carried a guitar for much of his American wanderings, never being reluctant to offer himself as an entertainer, especially if it meant a dollar or two coming his way. Regularly he now composed his own songs. Yet, lest it be taken that the lot of a troubadour is always carefree, there is one incident he relates in *Ploughman of the Moon* which rather poignantly lets us see that although he may at this time have been a drifter, he was not a down-and-out. On the road one day he befriended a young boy on his way home from school. The boy commented on his 'funny' way of speaking. To Service's explanation that he still retained something of a Scots accent, the boy replied that his family came from Ayrshire and his father was an avid reader of Burns. Then, 'What's your name, son?' 'Jimmy Service,' was the response, 'Why don't you come home with me and meet my folks?' One can sense fear more than embarrassment coming from Service as he declined the offer. Fear that home and the world might find out how he really was at that time.

It is commonplace in magazine articles written about Service's travelling years to see him referred to as a vagabond or hobo. This is to misunderstand the man. He may have rubbed shoulders with them but he was not of their ilk. Still less was he a vagrant. There was a wandering streak in him that had to be expurgated before he could come to terms with life, but its eradication did not demand that what the world still saw as honour and decency (those publicly acclaimed values of his Victorian upbringing) should be thrown to the winds. There might be stubble on his chin but he still clung to the values engrained by his home and school. One senses that, after his encounter with Jimmy Service he started, in his mind at least, to claw his way back to public respectability, although being sacked for incompetence as a dishwasher did not help his self-esteem.

The news that gold had been found on the Klondike did not stir him. If there was a lightness in his step as he crossed the great wild lands of Utah, Arizona and Colorado and moved into the beautiful cattle country of Nevada and Oregon it was because he had now made the decision to return to British Columbia. The odd jobs he was obliged to take on the way were sores to be suffered as he contemplated his return to conventional society.

Crossing the Tehachapi range he suffered a severe blow. Caught with a train behind him on a high trestle viaduct, in his scramble to safety he unhooked his pack and saw it, with his beloved guitar, plummet to the bottom of the gorge. It was the final straw. With all speed he now made for Vancouver Island, back to Cowichan Valley.

According to Jack Fleetwood, the distinguished citizen and notable Cowichan historian, when Service returned to Cowichan he lived first with the Mutter family and then with a Welshman called Harry Evans before once again taking up the duties of a cowman with the Corfields. He was happy to be working with stock and even happier after a few months when Corfield appointed him to take over the running of the store and Post Office which he owned. Service seemed to consider his job as a storeman an acknowledgement that he had returned to respectability, and certainly his return to the social scene is well recorded from this time on. But let us use his own words to describe his feelings at this time:

> Once again a white collar man. How happy I was! I wanted to sing and dance. On Monday I was hustling sixteen hours a day. On Tuesday I was watching others hustle and getting the same pay for it. Warm and dry I beheld another drive the stock to water, and tried to imagine that other was myself. It seemed too good to be true. Here I sat with the family, in a blue serge suit, eating in the dining-room, while through the intervening door of the kitchen I could see the farm hands in their grimy overalls gobbling down their food. For a long time, I am sorry to say, I got pleasure from this dolorous contrast. It is true that through the misery of others we appreciate our own well-being.

Service's relationship with the Corfield family must have been special. No longer sleeping in the bunk-house but in his own room above the store, he seems to have been a bit of a hero to the Corfield sons. In later years they were to recount their memories of 'the little red-faced Scotsman' who told them 'wild and woolly stories' up in the barn of their father's dairy farm. Somewhat

The seat memorial to Robert Service at Cowichan where he was
an active member of the tennis club

inevitably described by one of the sons as a loner, he went on to
say in an interview that wherever Service lived he made friends.

Much of the social life in Cowichan centred round the tennis
club. This club was formed only ten years after the formation
of the All-England Club at Wimbledon, and claims the double
fame of being the source of the game in Canada and of having
Service as a member. It is known that he habitually sat in the shade
of a particular maple in the club policies reading his dictionary.
His name appears in the centre of a teacloth which the ladies
of the club embroidered in 1901 showing the signatures of the
members.

But his interests at that time ranged far from tennis. He was
involved in the activities of St Peter's Anglican Church, which still
stands today, and pioneer woman Beatrice Day, who was to reach

her century, recalled that Service used to sing with her in the choir. Another Cowichan pioneer woman, Mary Marriner, remembered Service appearing in an operetta and insists he was known as a champion hand-shaker – a surprising comment, as Service considered handshaking a French and not a Scottish custom. The Shares, who certainly warranted the description of local society leaders, regularly had Service as a guest at their house parties. The first gramophone in Cowichan appears to have been bought by Corfield in 1901, adding another dimension to the tennis parties in a district said to be 'peopled by a very fast set, with sport as their God.' Certainly the women of Cowichan played a very full part in the development of the area, and in later years Service's tribute was to be incorporated in a memorial to them:

You will know you have played your part;
Yours shall be the love that never dies;
You, with Heaven's peace within your heart,
You, with God and Glory in your eyes.

Attracted as he was to the white collar status of the job, his entry into storekeeping required learning new skills. Much of his work involved trading with the Siwash Indians, so he had to learn Chinook, the medium which allowed communication between the various tribes and between tribe and colonist. Mail had to be sorted, milk taken to the creamery and the store books kept. Less pleasantly, he had to butcher and dress cattle and sheep, and in this he became extremely competent. But as a salesman his success was limited; with a sparkle of creativity he bedecked some chamber pots with ribbon and sold them to Indians as soup bowls, marriage presents, coffee urns or whatever an inquirer suggested they might be. For Service, the attractiveness of the job lay not in its content, but in the fact that it was a relatively cushy number, offering time for relaxation and entry into respectable society.

After three years of store life Service again suffered pangs of conscience. He was not getting anywhere, he was again a square peg in a round hole. Up in his little room at nights he would immerse himself in books, and the thought came to him that perhaps in some way the books he loved so much could become a greater part of his life. Perhaps he should become a teacher, or better, perhaps even a professor pontificating in front of an enthralled class. And as he dreamed, his ego fortified his ambition: his mind was made up; the route was charted; he would study for university matriculation.

It was Cunninghame Graham who maintained that failure was more interesting than success. By that definition, up to that time Service was an interesting character, and the mould was not to be broken. Full of good intentions, he buckled down to his new studies and saved as hard as he could in preparation for the scholastic life he now envisaged would be his lot.

When his capital reached two hundred dollars he handed in his notice to an almost unbelieving Corfield and moved to a peacefully located shack to devote himself completely to the required matriculation subjects. But if the spirit was willing the body was weak. It seemed as if the more he tried to amass knowledge, the more the ripple of the stream and the freshness of the mountain greenery sent out a Lorelei-like call drawing him from his studies and away to destruction. As a kind of mental compromise his mind turned to verse, and the elation of receiving five dollars for a poem dispatched to *Munsey's Magazine* did little to steel his dedication to his avowed goal.

The university entrance examinations were spread over three days and in some of the subjects, especially literature, he acquitted himself well. But failures in French and algebra necessitated further study, and by this time his funds were low. In a kind of dream, he found himself one day walking for miles, and then, when physically played out, with a callous indifference to logic, treated himself to a sumptuous and ridiculously expensive meal.

He was now aware that with his failure to matriculate there was more than a tinge of relief that he was not committing himself to a life of intellectual study. Yet, here he was at the age of thirty, a misfit, a dreamer, concerned about his future but with no star to follow. Dispirited, he was at the end of his tether.

And each forgets, as he strips and runs,
With a brilliant, fitful pace,
It's the steady, quiet, plodding ones
Who win in the lifelong race.
And each forgets that his youth has fled,
Forgets that his prime is past,
Till he stands one day with a hope that's dead
In the glare of the truth at last.

CHAPTER 3

Call of the Yukon

Never was seen such an army, pitiful, futile, unfit;
Never was seen such a spirit, manifold courage and grit;
Never has been such a cohort under one banner unrolled
As surged to the ragged-edged Arctic, urged by the arch-tempter – Gold.

The Trail of '98

SOME MEN MAINTAIN THAT a providential star stands over them; others, that the up-and-down events of their life are a planned prelude to the undertaking of some grand design. Was this the case with Service? One senses that in terms of morale he was now at his lowest ever point. His retreat from applying for university entrance had been followed by rejection for a job as a clerk. So, that was that; he was fed up with the farming life, unwanted in an office, desperate for respectability, and sick of work that seemed to get him nowhere. Never would he be in greater need of the mystic helping hand. On the surface, all he could offer a prospective employer was a tidy appearance and the reference given to

Robert Service wearing the 4-inch hard collar that was his standard bank dress

him all those years ago when he left the bank in Glasgow. As it was to turn out, that was sufficient.

In a dejected state, Service was standing outside the office of the Canadian Bank of Commerce in Victoria when he met a biscuit salesman he had known from his storekeeping days. After a few niceties about his health and what he was doing in Victoria, the salesman, with simple directness, encouraged him to walk into the Bank and ask for a job. With more timidity than temerity he acted on the advice. To his amazement he was offered a position in the Bank; even his offer to work for less than the stipulated salary was brushed aside. So, it was back to the desk grindstone, and he applied himself totally to becoming a valuable member of the bank staff.

His salary of fifty dollars a month allowed him to maintain a certain status. He was given a flat above the bank in which to live and undertake guard duties. He confessed that it would have taken an almighty explosion to waken him during the night, but being master of his own house meant he could hire a piano and play and sing his own songs to his heart's content. His social world now included the golf club. Not a sadder man but surely a wiser one, he was on the road to recovering the values his inner self deemed so important, no matter how he sought from time to time to subjugate them. After six months his salary was raised by ten dollars. It is not unfair to say that this strengthened his loyalty to the bank; certainly it reinforced his determination to make a success of his banking life.

Those who enter banking must accept job movements as standard practice, and Service could not have been too surprised when he was told he was being moved to the bank's office at Kamloops in central British Columbia.

In environmental terms, Victoria and Kamloops were far apart, and indeed still are. Victoria, very British, heavily timbered and temperate in climate: Kamloops, open and sparsely vegetated, cattle country with summer temperatures easily passing the hundred mark. Once again Service showed his ability to fit in to any company. He bought a pony, and although admitting he was averse to polo, developed a passion for riding. He got to know many of the ranchers well and would ride home in the early hours of the morning from their social functions. Stories of the happenings in the Yukon continued to pass him by. A new banjo was his friend and toy – his books were secondary. If not a workaholic, in today's parlance, there is no doubt the bank was the centre of his life. But if it was in truth a providential star that guided Service to the bank in Victoria where he was given employment, that star was to maintain an interest in where he should go.

One morning the branch manager called Service into his private office, and gave him the news that he was to be posted to the Whitehorse branch of the bank in the Yukon. Service, we can imagine, was taken aback – postings to the Yukon were much sought after, and his transfer was a sure indication that the bank valued him. And surely, with his restive nature, excitement must have been mixed with surprise. But it was the excitement associated with movement and a new experience, not excitement because of the possibility of striking it rich as a part-time gold miner.

Those given Yukon appointments were also given an outfit allowance, so the traditional coonskin coat was purchased as the travel arrangements were finalised. Towards the end of 1904, Robert William Service took ship for the Alaskan port of Skagway, the main gateway to the Yukon. Only the little star overhead could have known what fame and fortune lay ahead of him.

> We landed in wind-swept Skagway. We joined the weltering mass,
> Clamouring over their outfits, waiting to climb the Pass.
> We tightened our girths and our pack straps; we linked on the Human Chain,
> Struggling up to the summit, where every step was a pain.

The name of Service has become so inexorably linked with the Yukon (even today he is spoken of there with a remarkable reverence) that it is important to get an understanding of the environment he was now entering. And to do this it is best we go back in history some two score years before Service arrived in the Territory.

On the North American continent there have always been men fascinated by the search for precious metals. The first strikes which prompted 'rushes' were in Colorado, Nevada and California, but gradually the prospectors moved north, being followed in turn by those who made their livings and pickings from the gold camps; traders, prostitutes and gamblers. The gold trail headed into British Columbia. Then in 1880 gold was found near Juneau in Alaska and this town was in due course to become a springboard for further finds in the North. By the mid-1880s it was reckoned that some two hundred miners were prospecting or operating in the Yukon, that expanse of a hundred and eighty thousand square miles named after the river, which, springing into life a mere fifteen miles from the Pacific Ocean, flows a tortuous two thousand miles before entering salt water in the Bering Sea.

Pierre Berton, that doyen of Canadian journalists who was raised in the Yukon and who knows it as well as any man, gives a fascinating description in his book *Klondike* of the terrain which was to capture the world's imagination.

> There was gold on Atlin Lake at the very head of the Yukon River, and there was gold more than two thousand miles to the northwest in the glittering sands of the beach on Norton Sound into which the same river empties. There was gold on the Pelly and the Big Salmon and the Stewart, majestic water-courses that spill down from the Mackenzie Mountains of Canada to the East, and there was gold on the great Tanana, which rises in the Alaska range on the Southwest. There was gold in between these points at Minook and at Birch Creek and on the frothing Fortymile. Yet, compared with a wretched little salmon stream and its handful of scrawny creeks, these noble rivers meant little. For in the Klondike Valley gold lay more thickly than on any other creek, river pup, or sandbar in the whole of the Yukon watershed.

It was in the August of 1896 that George Washington Carmack and his two Indian companions, Skookum Jim and Tagish Charlie, discovered gold on the small Klondike tributary they called Rabbit Creek and which was later to be named Bonanza. They passed the word on to other prospectors they chanced to meet on the trail, and the news spread rapidly amongst their own kind. The extent of the discovery prompted the prospectors working in the Yukon Territory to make for the Klondike, where, according to hunch or imagined logic, they drove a wooden stake into the ground as a first step to recording a title to the land. But as these new diggings were nearly six hundred miles from the nearest coastal town of Skagway in Alaska, little information about the richness of the strike was to reach the outside world for some time. Indeed, it was not until the summer of the next year when the new millionaires unloaded their gold from the freighters which had carried them South from Skagway to Seattle and San Francisco that an astounded world realised to what extent the ground was giving up its riches.

Then started one of the greatest gold rushes in history as farmers and clerks, honest toilers and swindlers from the Americas, Europe and beyond, set out for the Yukon, their optimism refusing to accept the fact that the best claims had been registered months previously by men whose greater optimism had taken them into the North in the first place.

It is said that a hundred thousand men set out for the diggings. Although some of the more foolhardy tried the rugged overland trail from Edmonton by way of the Peace River, a journey of nearly two thousand miles that required an explorer's abilities, most opted to start by taking the steamer to Skagway or to the neighbouring township of Dyea further up the Taiya inlet. But finding space on a ship was the easy part of the journey. From Skagway or Dyea the stampeders had to carry their goods up either the White Pass from Skagway or the Chilkoot Pass from Dyea, a trek of over thirty miles.

The Mounties (North West Mounted Police was their title in

these days) would not allow anyone to cross the border into Canada unless they carried provisions for three months. This meant that, including equipment and tools, something in the order of a ton of goods per person had to be moved, and moved up steep slopes on a trail in places only wide enough to take one person. But the heart goes out most to the poor horses shipped up to Skagway and Dyea by people possessing no idea of the conditions which would be met.

Few would accuse the writer Jack London who also knew the area, of being tender-hearted, but he was to write:

> The horses died like mosquitoes in the first frost, and from Skagway to Bennett they rotted in heaps. They died at the rocks, they were poisoned at the summit, and they starved at the lakes; they fell off the trail, what there was of it, and they went through it; in the river they drowned under their loads or were smashed to pieces against the boulders; they snapped their legs in the crevices and broke their backs falling backwards with their packs; in the sloughs they sank from fright or smothered in the slime; and they were disembowelled in the bogs where the corduroy logs turned end up in the mud; men shot them, worked them to death and when they were gone, went back to the beach and bought more. Some did not bother to shoot them, stripping the saddles off and shoes and leaving them where they fell. Their hearts turned to stone – those which did not break – and they became beasts, the men on the Dead Horse Trail.

It is said that the carcasses of three thousand horses lay at the bottom of the place called Dead Horse Gulch on the White Pass. It was not only horses that died. The sub-arctic conditions, avalanches and cold took a deadly toll of the fortune seekers in the unbroken single file which stretched up both the passes to Lake Lindeman or Lake Bennett. And because each stampeder had to move his ton of goods on a cache-to-cache basis, this meant many repeated journeys involving hundreds of miles of trudging in the human chain. The journey in total could take up to three months. Murders and suicides were common. Even today, a hundred years

Scenes from the Yukon

after the event, those walking the passes can pick up kit discarded by the would-be miners as they sought to lighten their loads.

Their troubles were not over when those who sought the gold arrived at the lake. Then they had to build boats to take themselves and their chattels the six hundred miles to the settlement that was becoming Dawson City. Ahead of them lay such perils as Miles Canyon with its whirlpool, and the jagged rocks of White Horse and Five-finger and other rapids. In one day alone, over a hundred boats were wrecked and ten men drowned. Again, it was a race against other stampeders if a likely claim was to be staked, with the starting gun being the break-up of the ice.

Within forty-eight hours of the ice moving in the late spring of 1897, over seven thousand boats built by those seekers for gold took off from the shores of Lake Bennett and Lake Lindeman in one of the craziest armadas the world has ever seen. And the next year there was to be no let up in the mad rush to reach the Klondike.

In his wonderful narrative poem, *The Trail of Ninety-Eight*, Service was to capture completely the fierce challenge of the journey by water down to Dawson:

> We built our boats and we launched them.
> Never has been such a fleet,
> A packing case for a bottom, a mackinaw for a sheet.
> Shapeless, grotesque, lopsided, flimsy, makeshift and crude;
> Each man after his fashion builded as best he could.
> Dared we that ravening terror; heard we its din in our ears;
> Called on the Gods of our fathers, juggled forlorn with our fears;
> Sank to our waists in its fury, tossed to the sky like a fleece;
> Then, when our dread was the greatest, crashed into safety and peace.

By the time Service received his bank posting to the Yukon the mad rush for gold was over. Some disillusioned prospectors had already made for home or had followed the gold trail into Alaska. Service's first Yukon posting was not to Dawson but to the township of Whitehorse, some three hundred and fifty miles to the

South. In later years, Whitehorse would overtake Dawson in size and become the capital of the Territory with a population of fourteen thousand, but in 1904 it contained all the elements of a frontier existence. While providing feeder services to the more Northern gold fields, it possessed a distinct trapping and trading culture. But Whitehorse was on the route to Dawson and if Service travelled there with more comfort than the stampeders enjoyed, nature would ensure the journey would not lack interest.

The sea journey to Skagway, by way of the inside passage, which Service was now to take, is possibly the most dramatic ferry route in the world. Protected from the worst of the Pacific swell by a string of islands stretching from Vancouver and the Charlottes in the South to the Alexander Archipelago off the Alaskan Panhandle in the North, the traveller from start to finish relishes a feast of interest. The ports of call provide remarkably diverse fascinations. Ketchican, the salmon capital of the world, boasts the world's largest collection of totem poles; Petersburg residents advertise their Scandinavian cultural heritage with decorative 'rosemaling' on houses and shop fronts. The still active Russian churches in Juneau and Sitka are a reminder that Alaska once belonged to that great country across the Bering sea. The hordes of bald eagles to be seen in the vicinity of Haines; the spouting of humpback and the black and white orca whales, the blue-coloured brilliance of the vast glaciers, the humorous misshapes of the ice floes in turquoise waters – all these ensure that the journey is, in Service's words, 'one of wonder and joy.' For the Yukon-bound, the ferry's journey today ends at Skagway, where, thanks to various private, State and Federal initiatives, the town is much the same as it was a hundred years ago: the broadwalks and false-fronted buildings, the rooms of the Arctic Brotherhood and the old spit-and-sawdust saloons evoke the atmosphere of the gold rush era.

Service was spared the trek up the White Pass and the ordeal of a scow journey to Whitehorse. A narrow-gauge railway had been built from Skagway, which, because of its clinging to incredible rock faces like a limpet and the sheer awesomeness of the terrain it traversed, was to become one of the world's great train journeys. Service, though, saw little. Snow was falling and the windows were largely opaque with ice. But what he did see was enough to ensure that for the rest of his life he admired those who had taken the trail of 'ninety-eight. As the train climbed to the timber line and moved through Tormentation Valley, the stunted and sparse vegetation and the cruel crags blackening the snow, which apparently stretched to eternity, brought home the realisation that here was a land that could only be lived in by a special breed of men and women. From the railway halt at Carcross down to Whitehorse the line follows some of the most strikingly beautiful scenery in the Yukon: with this land Service was soon to be on intimate terms.

The humour he expressed on reaching journey's end seemed to establish the happiness that was to be his over the next three years: 'As I stepped on to the Whitehorse platform it seemed jammed with coonskin coats. But for the rosy faces of the men inside them, it might have been a coon carnival'.

Service accepted the invitation to live in the home of his new branch manager. The DeGex's were a charming couple, and together with a teller from the bank of Service's own age who also lived in the house, a tight, harmonious group was soon formed. During the long winter season business was quiet in the bank, and Service used much of the generous spare time given to him to explore both the trails around Whitehorse and the social distractions of the town. Then, as winter faded and the snow disappeared, his life changed dramatically. Workers poured in for the summer months, and the pilots and crews of the sternwheelers now built to operate on the Yukon river appeared. Life in the bank became hectic as the community tried to cram a year's work into four months. Mining had to be done, and goods had to be shipped in and out of the territory before the freeze returned. It is not difficult to decide which season Service preferred.

When the great cold came to the Yukon it clamped the land tight as a drum. The transient scurried out, and the residents squatted snugly in. They were the sourdoughs; the land belonged to them; the others were but parasites living on its bounty. That is what we felt as we settled down to the Long Night. It was a comfortable feeling to be shut off from the world with its woes and worries; for we had few of the first and none of the latter. In the High North, winter is long, lonely and cruelly cold, but to the sourdough it is the season best beloved. For then he makes for himself a world of his own, full of happy, helpful people. The Wild brings out virtues we do not find easily in cities – brotherhood, sympathy, high honesty. As if to combat the harshness of Nature, human nature makes an effort to be at its best.

There are two things well worth noting about Service at this time. First, at the age of thirty he could be described as fit and clean. Seldom more than an occasional drinker, he would claim liquor never passed his lips for the three years he was to serve the bank in Whitehorse. Nor could it be said that he had a fondness for the ladies – a bonus for anyone posted to the Yukon, where they were not over-plentiful. Such contacts as he had with the opposite sex always seemed to be on a very proper basis. He maintained a diffidence in manner. He projected mildness: indeed, over the years people were to find it difficult to reconcile the man and the legend. In dress he could be described as dapper. Captain T. V. Fleming, who served as a constable in the North West Mounted Police in Whitehorse, and who knew Service well, once recalled that he was never seen without a stiff collar about six inches high. The image of the Scots banker, it would seem, was not considered inappropriate in a different clime. And exercise with Service was a crusade; walking a kind of drug to be taken in large doses. But walking in the Yukon, even when snowshoes are not necessary, must not be confused with strolling down leafy lanes in a more gentle climate. It was a dangerous occupation. The chances of getting lost in the timber were ever present; it is a country populated by grizzly bears and huge moose still to-day claiming victims from time to time. Such walking as Service did then provided more than exercise: it provided atmosphere and background for the tales that were to come. In his own words:

> With lunch in my pocket, I would go for the entire day on snow-shoes, striking across the river and exploring the snowy waste beyond. I would break trail under the pines, feeling supremely alone in the dazzling solitude and filled with a rapture I have rarely known. It was then I realised the poetry of my surroundings, but did not yet dream of trying to put it into words. I just felt it with that inarticulate sense people feel in the presence of serene beauty. But I most loved the woods in the silver trance of the moon. The moon seemed my friend, calling on me to express the rapture that flooded me.

The second point about Service is especially important as it was to prompt him towards his future. Although always one who enjoyed his own company, he relished being in a position to entertain others, to be a centre of attraction. It is not an unusual streak; many of us can think of the shy, silent individual who, perhaps with a little encouragement from alcohol, becomes the star of a party. Service had regularly been involved in amateur dramatics, had composed verse and songs and played a number of instruments. At this time, with a little pressure from his boss, he was serving as a deacon in the Episcopalian church in Whitehorse. Minutes of meetings written up by Service are still in the church archives today.

This church, of course, is most famous for its adventurous minister, Bishop Stringer, surely the only man of the cloth ever to have eaten his boots! Stringer got caught in a snowstorm between Fort McPherson and Dawson on what was known as the Edmonton trail – a trail that had the reputation of killing half the men who challenged it. Unable to go on because of the blinding snow, his provisions used up, Stringer decided to eat his boots, which had walrus-leather soles and sealskin tops. He boiled the boots for seven hours before baking them on hot stones.

Afterwards the Bishop was to describe his sustenance as, 'tough and stringy, but palatable and satisfying.' He was ultimately saved, the ordeal having cost him fifty pounds in weight.

Saturday evenings frequently saw Service in the church hall taking part in the home-made entertainment. His speciality seems to have been recitation, but as he confesses, his *Gunga Din* and *The Face on the Bar-room Floor* were getting stale with repetition. He wrote short plays for local performance. In one, Captain Fleming had to play the part of a young girl. The mountie obtained some necessary accessories from a lady friend and the two men returned to a flat above the bank where Service applied make-up to his friend's face before the performance. For reasons of security, recalled Fleming, every room was brightly lit and every curtain drawn back. Next day, all round the town, was a dreadful scandal about how a member of the bank staff had been seen behaving most disgracefully with a woman.

Stroller White, the editor of *The White Horse Star*, frequently printed some of Service's verse, and it was his suggestion that Service write something with local colour for a forthcoming concert. It was a seed planted in the right soil at the right time. On his walks he would search for a suitable theme, and one night it came to him. He was leaving the woods to enter Whitehorse when he heard the sounds of revelry coming from a number of bars. Into his mind jumped the phrase, *A bunch of the boys were whooping it up*. From there on things happened at speed. To give himself privacy he by-passed the house and made for the bank where he settled down at his desk. The plot of his story unfolded as he worked into the small hours of the morning. By five o'clock his first great narrative poem had been completed. 'It came easy,' he later recalled, 'it was as if someone was whispering in my ear.' Little did he know he had just written something that would be recited with great gusto by many thousands of men, women and children over the years ahead.

There is a curious parallel here between *The Shooting of Dan McGrew*, which is the best known and loved of Service's poems, and *Tam O'Shanter*, the best known and loved of Robert Burns's work. It appears that both were written in one marathon session of composition. Both were produced at the instigation of another person. Both achieved a popularity certainly quite unmatched in English language poetry. And surely both are immortal. If those two poets had written nothing but those two masterpieces, each would be still remembered and loved, and deservedly so.

We all know:

> A bunch of the boys were whooping it up in the Malamute saloon;
> The kid that handles the music box was hitting a ragtime tune;
> Back of the bar, in a solo game, sat Dangerous Dan McGrew,
> And watching his luck was his light-o'-love, the lady that's known as Lou.

The peculiar twist to the story of the gunfight over the lady known as Lou is that Service did not recite it at the church social – he was afraid that its robust nature might give offence to some of the ladies who would be present. So, into a drawer it went, although it was not to remain alone for long. A few weeks later he picked up a story from a miner and it completely captivated him. This yarn matured in his mind as he walked the trails in the moonlight. From his bank ledger he appropriated the name 'McGee' for the hero of his saga, and when that great story was written down, it joined *Dan McGrew* in the bureau drawer.

> There are strange things done in the midnight sun
> By the men who moil for gold;
> The Arctic trails have their secret tales
> That would make your blood run cold;
> The Northern Lights have seen queer sights,
> But the queerest they ever did see
> Was the night on the marge of Lake Lebarge
> I cremated Sam McGee.

The real Sam McGee (for the tale had a kernel of truth), as his daughter was later to point out, never had any connection with

Tennessee – a point of little importance to a rhymster – but his immaculately-kept cabin sits today within the compound of the Whitehorse museum. The Yukon air is so dry that the contents of cabins do not readily disintegrate or rust.

Pierre Berton in his introduction to Ted Harrison's beautifully illustrated book on the poem, makes the point that *Sam McGee* is authentic Yukon while *Dan McGrew* is an American Wild West tale. Sam McGee belongs to the North; it deals with the cold, so familiar to all Yukoners, although there is nothing but warmth in tale itself:

> And there sat Sam,
> looking cool and calm, in the heart of the furnace roar;
> And he wore a smile you could see a mile, and he said:
> 'Please close that door.
> It's fine in here,
> but I greatly fear you'll let in the cold and storm –
> Since I left Plumtree, down in Tennessee,
> It's the first time I've been warm.'

By now the muse was truly within Service as verse followed verse: inspiration came from all sources; Miles Canyon prompted *Naked Grandeur*, *Call of the Wild* came from White Horse Rapids. To the lone figure plodding on snowshoes under the starry skies there seemed to be no end to the descriptive pieces he could write. It was as if the very landscape was speaking to him, urging him on to fill that drawer in his room with the very spirit of the Yukon. And from the fierce nature of the land, he turned to the raw nature and life of the mining camps. 'Vice,' he said, 'seemed to me a more vital subject for poetry than virtue.'

Even the most reluctant of observers could not miss the vice and bawdiness of Whitehorse at that time. The harshness of the life swiftly separated the men from the boys, and those that came to the fore were characters with traits and colour Service could readily seize upon. Thus, from his pen flowed gems of nature in

Miles Canyon in the Yukon. A prominent obstacle to those making their way
to the Klondike by boat. A favourite visiting place of the bard

the raw, but generally tempered to show that goodness is not the sole prerogative of the godly nor philosophy a monopoly of the educated. For a full two months Service was to write at speed, his faculties at a peak, his enthusiasm unabated. Then, almost as suddenly as it had arrived, the urge to write left him. The final sheets of manuscript were tumbled into the drawer. Once again his dislike of work took over; his respect for what he had written was diluted.

It was some months later that Mrs DeGex proffered the suggestion that he publish his collection of verse as Christmas presents to his friends. He had just been given a bonus from the bank and the idea appealed to the egotistic streak which was at the fore at the time. He decided he would get books printed to the value of the bonus. He claimed he regretted his conceit as soon as the package was posted.

CHAPTER 4

The Inspired Rhymster

Have you known the great white silence, not a snow-gemmed twig a-
    quiver?
(Eternal truths that shame our soothing lies.)
Have you broken trail on snowshoes? Mushed huskies up the river,
Dared the unknown, led the way, and clutched the prize?

Call of the Wild

THERE ARE FEW MORE bamboozling experiences in life than success landing on the doorstep when derision is expected. It is far
more confusing than anticipated success being replaced by failure
– that is a regular occurrence in life.

Service read the letter from the publisher with total disbelief.
Not only did it contain the request to publish his poems on a ten
per cent royalty basis, but there was a description of how the staff
and the salesman in the publishing company had shown incredible
enthusiasm for his work. Indeed, the salesman had already sold
seventeen hundred copies on the strength of the galley proofs.
Accepting the offered terms was the easy bit. What was difficult
was reconciling himself to a proven achievement – becoming
something of a local celebrity as word percolated through from
the outside world of his soaring book sales, and speaking to the
visitors who would come into the bank asking him to autograph
the book of his poems they had bought.

Not all reaction was good. The chief deacon at the church told
him 'My wife's been reading your book and she and the ladies of
the sewing circle think it is a pity you should have written so much
about the bad women of the town and said nothing about the
good ones.' His response that the good ones were taken for grant-

ed brought only a silence, but within himself he felt good, proud that he had achieved something which would leave his mark on the trail. The plaudits of others and the cheques that were to flutter occasionally through the letter box were, so far as he was concerned, a short-term bonus.

But the popularity of his first book of verse was not to diminish. More and more visitors wished to see the rhyming bank clerk who had tales to tell of the Yukon, working at his place behind the bank counter. It seemed as if he was the main tourist attraction Whitehorse offered. The embarrassment he felt as customers quoted his verse and ladies demonstrated an interest in his literary gifts, was not mollified by the glee at his predicament shown by his colleagues. Thankfully he welcomed the white mantle of snow as it returned to cover the land he loved so much. As the temperature dropped, the visitors and transient workers returned to the outside: the ties on the snowshoes were checked, and as a replete man settles, at peace with the world, to sleep in his chair by the fire, so the Yukoners relaxed into their winter of peace and long nights.

Service, though, was not to spend his third Yukon winter in Whitehorse. Leave was due to him and he returned to British Columbia. Then, instead of returning him to Whitehorse, the Bank of Commerce decided to post him to its Dawson branch. That indeed was good news. He had been worried that he might not be sent back to the Yukon, and he knew within himself that there was more he had to write about the North.

What he wanted above all was to get the feel of the Klondike, the aura, the ambience of the diggings, the legends, the memories of those who did and those who didn't strike it rich. His stay in Whitehorse had given him an intimacy with the Yukon as a territory. Now he was after the special world which existed within that massive land. So, once again the journey by water and land was undertaken. This time, though, it was to continue on for nearly another four hundred miles.

Here was my land, the grandest on earth, and it was welcoming me home. I would be its interpreter because I was at one with it. And this feeling has never left me. The Yukon was the source of my first real inspiration.

From Whitehorse to Dawson was six days by open sleigh. It was then I realised the vastness of the land and its unconquerable reservation. The temperature was about thirty below zero. With bells jingling, we swept through a fairyland of crystalline loveliness, each pine bough freighted with lace and gems, and a stillness that made silence seem like sound.

Our breath froze on our fur collars; our lashes and eyebrows were hoar; our cheeks pinky bright, as we took shallow breaths of the Arctic air. Every now and then the driver would have to break icicles out of the nostrils of his horses. Sometimes the sleigh would upset and often we would have to get out and push through waist-high snowdrifts. Twice a day we stopped at roadhouses to change horses. There we would find a meal prepared and be obliged to eat. Meals and beds cost two dollars each. When we woke up in the morning we would say 'Six o'clock, six dollars.'

With a population of over four thousand, Dawson at that time was much bigger than Whitehorse. The bank too was bigger, with the buying and shipping of gold dust and nuggets being part and parcel of the days work. After the warm civilised atmosphere of the bank house, Service found himself living in the log cabin which did duty as the mess for the bank's young employees. And it was a robust mess life, music and alcohol being the catalysts which ensured it was a centre of social life. The presence next door of the Mounted Police barracks meant that visitors were continually dropping in for a drink and contributing a yarn about the 'mounties' in the North.

Service settled into this arena of good-humoured rowdyism, accepting with good grace the unkind adjectives used to describe him as a bard. At work he applied himself diligently. With a sense

Offices of the Arctic Brotherhood. Service joined the Brotherhood and gained many stories from its members

of mission he set out to save as much money as he could, cultivating, as he put it, 'thrift to the point of frugality.' His habit of walking by himself late at night stayed with him, but as well as the trails, he liked to ramble round Dawson, looking at the buildings now standing empty, imagining the scenes they witnessed just a few years earlier when the gold rush was at its peak. He joined the Arctic Brotherhood, that fraternity of the North which provided him with the company of many who had hit the trail of 'ninety-eight. In their company, he admitted to being like a reporter, seeking to ferret out information that would provide a story. And, important for his own future, he realised no other writer was giving the world the true and colourful story of what had transpired in the North since George Carmack made his discovery in Rabbit Creek.

Laura Berton who was to get to know Service fairly well in Dawson, describes in her book *I Married the Klondike* her first impression of the bard whose reputation had preceded him:

He slid into town one day without any great fanfare, and was soon to be seen weighing out gold dust in the tellers' cage of the Canadian Bank of Commerce on Front Street. By this time his first and most famous book of poems, *Songs of a Sourdough*, was on everybody's lips and the whole camp was reciting *The Shooting of Dan McGrew*, *The Cremation of Sam McGee* and The Spell of the Yukon.

Miss Hamtorf and I, having missed Service in Whitehorse, immediately made a hurried excuse to turn up at the bank for a glimpse of the man whose poems we had already committed to memory. We had thought of him as a rip-roaring roisterer, but instead we found a shy and nondescript man in his mid thirties, with a fresh complexion, clear blue eyes and a boyish figure that made him look younger. He had a soft, well-modulated voice and spoke with a slight drawl, an English inflection, an American drawl and Scottish overtones.

[When Laura Berton wrote her magnificent story of the Yukon in her later years. Robert Service provided the preface to the book.]

That first summer in Dawson, Service had little time to put pen to paper. But as the snow fell, so he returned to his versifying, determined to get his second book out as soon as possible. Many will know the problem of trying to study with a young family in the house. Service's problem was the noise originating from a wild bunch of colleagues. Only in the early hours could he obtain quiet: so, it was to bed at nine where he would lie until midnight, then, after a pot of strong tea, he would concentrate and write until three in the morning. It was hard work writing without the benign presence of the spirit which had helped him with his first book. A letter to a friend written at this time indicates it was not only the noise that irritated him: he still possessed an anti-work complex.

Dawson Y.T. 14th June 1909
– I am still plugging away at the old job and likely to remain at it for some more years yet. I am teller here and have a pretty easy time.

> The drudgery of everything gets on my nerves and I envy you work-
> ing in God's good sunshine and able to snap your fingers at the
> world. I have made my literary debut and doing awfully well finan-
> cially but it's too hard satisfying both the Bank and one's publisher.
> I am publishing another book this coming Spring.

Four months later, the *Ballads of a Cheechako* was finished and dispatched to his publisher. To the amazement of Service, the publisher expressed nervousness about it, and there was an acrimonious correspondence before it finally went into print. There was no need for concern. The reek of reality rising from its pages would ensure its success. Within a short time he was to receive a cheque for three thousand dollars. Once again the public had declared it liked its heroes to be robust; and with Pious Pete, Claw-fingered Kitty, Blasphemous Bill and One-eyed Mike, they got what they wanted. So too did the upholders of law and order:

> Knights of the lists of unrenown, born of the frontier's need,
> Disdainful of the spoken word, exultant in the deed;
> Unconscious heroes of the waste, proud players of the game,
> Props of the power behind the throne, upholders of the name;
> For thus the great white chief hath said, 'In all my lands be peace',
> And to maintain his word he gave his West the Scarlet Police.

With two books to his credit, Service rested on his laurels. He suffered that aversion to writing known to many servants of the pen. He turned to the more social aspects of Dawson life: skating, snowshoe parties, bob-sleighing, dancing. 'I did everything,' he said, 'except curl, drink whisky and play poker.' He returned to amateur dramatics and church hall entertaining. Away from the bank he was gloriously happy. Work he tolerated, and he was grateful that as Dawson continued to decline, so the work in the bank became less arduous.

It was well over a year after his second book had been published that the urge to write again began to gnaw within him. This time, though, it was prose rather than verse that was capturing his imagination. He knew the Yukon; more important, he knew its characters, and what they had suffered to reach the diggings. He was both an astute observer and a patient, absorbing listener. His head was full of sourdough stories and tales that had taken on the aura of legends. Who, he pondered, was better equipped than he, to tell the story of the Klondike in novel form?

In any study of Service's life, the suggestion must surface that he was watched over by a benevolent star – events so often just seemed to fall into place. One even gets the impression that he acknowledged the 'divinity that shapes our ends, rough-hew them how we will.' He possessed a story, and the confidence, with two successful books to his credit, to write it with assurance. Yet, as he records, words came only with difficulty. Something was wrong. It did not take much thought to reach the conclusion that his surroundings were not conducive to literary effort. To write a novel he needed peace and seclusion, commodities somewhat scarce in the bank mess. Laura Berton had views on his need for company:

> He was a good mixer among men and spent a lot of time with the sourdoughs, but we could never get him to any of our parties. 'I'm not a party man,' he would say. 'Ask me sometime when you're by yourselves.' He seldom attended the various receptions or dinner-parties or Government House affairs which went on unceasingly, and soon people got out of the habit of inviting him. I remember how Earl Grey, the Governor-General of Canada, on a visit to Dawson, electrified the town by asking why Service hadn't been included among the guests at a reception. We had all forgotten how important the poet was.

And did providence have an interest in his future? One morning the bank manager called Service into his private office, to tell him he was being promoted to deputy manager at his old bank at Whitehorse, where his early presence was required. The first feeling of pride was quickly overtaken by one of dismay. Authority was not for him and he knew it. And such a move must set back the writing of his novel. He was at a cross-roads and a decision was required. To an astonished bank manager he blurted out that he could not take the appointment as he intended resigning from the bank to devote himself to writing. Perhaps, with a royalty income that was five times his bank salary, it was a decision he should have taken sooner. That it wasn't can be taken as an indication of how badly he needed to feel the security and respectability that the bank gave him.

His resignation meant that he had to find other accommodation. The cabin he moved into was on a hillside looking over the valley of the Yukon. It stands today as it stood then with the moose horns above the door extended like welcoming arms. His autobiography indicates pride of ownership:

The bard striking a dramatic pose outside his Dawson Cabin

The cabin was of logs with a porch on which I slung a hammock. There was a sitting-room and a bedroom, both furnished with monastic simplicity. The sittingroom had a small table, two chairs and a stove. The draught in the stove was so good I could light a fire in two minutes, and in ten the sides would be glowing red; then I could choke it off so that it would burn for ten hours. I heated water on the stove for tea but I took my meals out. I hung my photos on the wall, bought blankets, flannelette sheets and some cushions. I had the sitting-room painted a pale blue and a double door put on. Everything was snug and shipshape in what was to be my home for two years.

Service's new-found freedom was initially too much to his liking. Before he could start his novel he had to adjust his working hours, and a weakness for the bohemian existence came to the fore. He seldom rose before eleven, exercised, breakfasted on ham and eggs in a bakery kept by a Norwegian, played his guitar, then took to the trail before finishing his day with a book or yarning with a crony. For company he obtained a cat and a Siberian Bearhound, the largest dog in the Yukon, some said. But gradually a work routine emerged, and as the plot developed in his mind and on paper, so the book took over his whole being. Everything else became secondary. The winter months passed and his papers, drafts, corrections and the finished product occupied every available surface, including the floor.

The book was given the title *The Trail of '98* and, written in the first person, told the story of a young Scot, Athol Meldrum, who makes his way to North America and thence joins the company of those seduced by the lust for gold. Service filled the book with characters that were as robust as they come. The men in the book register with the reader but the heroine Berna, named, he later confessed, after a brand of condensed milk, makes less impact. His enthusiasm is most marked as he introduces authenticity into his tough characters, who are seldom completely bad:

'I'm Jim Hubbard, known as Salvation Jim, and I know minin' from Genesis to Revelation. Once I used to gamble an' drink the limit. One morning I got up from the card-table after sitting there thirty six hours. I'd lost five thousand dollars. I knew they'd handed me out cold turkey, but I took my medicine.

'Right then I said I'd be a crook too. I learned to play with marked cards. I could tell every card in the deck. I ran a stud-poker game, with a Jap an' a Chinaman for partners. They were quicker than white men, an' less likely to lose their nerve. It was easy money, like taking candy from a kid. Often I would play on the square. No man can bluff strong without showing it. Maybe it's just a quiver of the eyelash, maybe a shuffle of the foot. I've studied a man for a month till I found the sign that gave him away. Then I've raised and raised him till the sweat pricked through his brow. He was my meat'.

As the ice melted Service finished his first novel. A publisher in New York was already committed to take the book and as he parcelled up the manuscript the fear entered his head, 'What would he do if it got lost on its way to the big city?' Perhaps it was an inevitable response to a period of confinement. He decided to deliver it personally, and booked his passage to the coast.

Any fears he had at the time about the success of the novel were unfounded. It was to become a best-seller, and in later years find favour with Hollywood.

Service dallied for only a short time in Vancouver before starting his transcontinental rail journey. He did, though, in that most British of Canadian cities, meet another Scot of literary prowess who shared his love of travel and adventure.

Robert Bruce Lockhart was on his way home from Malaya to recuperate from malaria. Seven years junior to Service, Lockhart was, within a decade, to achieve substantial fame when circumstances not only made him 'our man in Moscow' during the Bolshevik revolution in 1917, but also saw him placed in solitary confinement in the Kremlin as a suspected counter-revolutionary. In his *Memoirs of a British Agent*, Sir Robert, as he was to become, recalls:

> When we arrived in Vancouver, I was introduced to Robert Service, and for the first time in months blood came back to my cheeks. I was a shy youth and could still blush, and Service, then at the height of his fame, was the first British author I had met. He gave me autographed copies of his *Songs of a Sourdough* and his *Ballads of a Cheechako*. Today, with the rest of my books, they are doubtless gracing the shelves of a Bolshevik library, unless, which is highly probable, they have been burnt by the Moscow hangman as imperialistic effluvia, and, therefore, noxious to Moscow nostrils.

Service arrived in New York to stay at the National Arts Club on the invitation of an artist he had met in the Yukon. The sumptuousness of his surroundings merely served to emphasise the extent to which he had been 'Yukonised'. Unattracted to high living and devoid of sophistication, he sought his pleasures in a music hall in the Bowery, the only part of New York he really liked. He was like a fish out of water.

To his publishers he seemed too mild to be a hero of the Yukon; to himself he felt too ordinary to be at home amongst the glitter of the big city. When his business with his publisher was over he made one of his spontaneous decisions. He wanted colour not concrete. He would make for New Orleans by the mode of travel he was most comfortable with – walking. But it was neither walking country nor walking weather, and after a few days he became disillusioned, and completed the journey by train. New Orleans only partly quenched his desire for colour and with something akin to despondency he booked passage for Cuba.

Cuba probably gave Service the simple enjoyment he was needing at that time. The bustle of America had disturbed his equilibrium. Sitting in a street cafe in Havana he could once again be the onlooker seeing most of the game. As he was to write in his autobiography:

> Yes, picturesque dirt, idleness, procrastination, I'll accept all that for the freedom, the glamour that goes with it. Let the Nordics sweep their stables speckless, give me the Latin way of living. And today I feel the same. I suppose it is the spirit of the gypsy. I prefer the thymy Thea hills to the regimented tulip gardens of Holland. Let me live in slip-shod loveliness where pleasures are many and duties are few.

Unfortunately life seldom accommodates perfectly. As Service enjoyed the indolence, so his girth responded in an unbecoming way. The fitness fanatic within him revolted at the sight of his paunchiness, but the mañana ambience of the place held him fast.

The novelty of the situation, the freshness and verve of the guitar playing, he admitted, kept him rooted to the cafe life. His longing for colour took him into the less salubrious parts of Havana, where he encouraged a rather evil-looking guitarist to give him lessons playing flamenco style.

In a bid to return his body to its former hardness he decided to walk to Santiago, but a few days on the open road in the humid heat, coupled with poor accommodation, was too much for him in his unfit condition, and he returned to Havana. He lounged for a while longer, but one senses that boredom was setting in. He had difficulty in getting reading material: he tired of the incessant sun. The voice of the North came to him, urging him home. He packed his valise for the journey.

In *Ploughman of the Moon* Service makes little reference to his family after bidding them goodbye in Glasgow. It appears, though, that he was not the only member of his family to be attracted to the farming life in Canada. Which one of his brothers or sisters or parents had articulated the suggestion or taken the initiative is not known, but a few years after Service had emigrated to Vancouver Island, the family pulled up their roots and made for Alberta, where they obtained a small farm in an area well peopled with Scots. It was a pioneer existence, but it seemed to give Mrs Service a new lease of life, and she became the driving force of the family. And as Service determined to return to the Yukon, the mood took him to visit his family on the way. As he put it, 'I would do a prodigal son in reverse.'

This he did, and it was a welcome reunion, seeing the faces he had not seen for many years. It was winter-time and he snugly returned to the family circle, helping with the chores about the place, inevitably walking, and in one traumatic experience, help-ing to defend the farmhouse against a prairie fire which threatened to engulf it. But the warmth of the family circle was not lure enough to keep him in Alberta. As the snow melted, the call of the High North became stronger, and he made ready to move.

This time he would deny himself the modest comforts of the

Inside Passage and being driven in a horse sleigh. He would return to Dawson using the old Edmonton Trail, the trail which had broken so many who had ventured its way. It meant the traversing of more than two thousand miles of wilderness, the lifeline being the trading posts of the Hudson Bay Company, normally factored by Hebrideans or Orcadians, and each far apart from its neighbour. He assessed the fifty-fifty odds as favourable. It was as if having proved himself as a writer, there was a need to show the world he was a true figure of the North. After this journey, there would be no doubt about that.

Service made for Edmonton, where he picked up the stage-coach for the two-day journey to Athabasca Landing. The barges of the Hudson Bay Company had left two days earlier on their trip down the Athabasca to replenish their traders' stores, so, obtaining a canoe and an Indian guide, Service took off in pursuit. The canoeing was hard work and it was another three days before they caught up with the company's fleet.

This was oil country, and Service recounts passing a flaming

The author at the plaque to Robert Service outside the
Bank of Commerce at Whitehorse

jet of natural gas which had apparently been burning for twenty-five years. But all he had to do now was enjoy the sail down the river and the monstrous meals served up by the cook.

The arrival at Fort MacMurray he likened to a carnival as the whisky-starved population celebrated the end of their long months of isolation. With anticipation he took up residence in the state-room of the steamer that during the next two weeks would take him down the rest of the Athabasca and then the Slave river to Smith's Landing. His anticipation was marred only by the Indian Agent telling him his plans would lead to his doom.

At Smith's Landing a twenty mile portage had to be made because of rapids, and then he boarded another steamer at Fort Smith which would take him down to Fort Simpson. This part of the journey was special to him, as it was here he became the owner of he claimed, the finest birch-bark canoe in the North:

> I bought it at Great Slave Lake from an old Indian who was consid-
> ered the best canoe-maker of his tribe. He judged it a masterpiece
> and truly, it was like a flame upon the water. A gaudy patchwork of
> purple, scarlet, primrose and silver, it danced on the ripple as lightly
> as a leaf. The old man sighed as he parted with it. He had gone far
> to select the bark. He had sewn it with wood fibre and lashed it with
> willow wands. It had taken him a year to fashion, and now he looked
> at it with the sadness of an artist who sees his finest work being
> sold. With reluctance, he took the twenty-five dollars I offered him.

Service continued on the steamer down the giant Mackenzie River, stopping regularly at the Bay posts. At one point he accompanied some mounties as they investigated an incident where two former trappers in partnership had fallen out and killed each other, a reminder to him of the peculiar strains associated with living a life of solitude. Indeed, Service always maintained the Mackenzie was more murderous than the Yukon, its law harder and its tribute higher. Most of the men he knew on the Mackenzie were to be killed in one way or another.

The end of the steamer journey was at Fort Macpherson, where the Peel River joined the Mackenzie. By now he was well within the Arctic Circle. After clearing its load, the steamer would return up-river picking up pelts from the forts it had supplied with provisions on its way north. The old factor at Fort Macpherson had read some of his books. But as he sold Service his provisions came the advice, 'Don't go on. Go back the way you came like a good little boy.' The officer of the mounties gave the same advice. Ignoring the advice, he set up his tent with some Eskimos. He exchanged presents with the chief. In return for a fish-hook of walrus ivory he gave his safety razor: he reckoned if he was to blaze a trail to the Yukon, he would be more in character with a beard.

Service's intention was to carry his canoe across the Great Divide before making his way down the Bell and the Porcupine to the Yukon River where he would paddle upstream to Dawson. He had expected to find Indians who would help him to carry his canoe and stores the hundred miles over the Divide. In this he was disappointed, although he offered generous payment. Then he fell in with company as unconventional as himself.

Captain McTosh and Jake Skilly were true men of the North, capable of living where others would die. Implacable foes of the Hudson's Bay Company, they were long-time trappers on the Mackenzie Delta. And now they too were inspired to take their scow over the Great Divide and make for Dawson. McTosh was accompanied by his wife, and it was agreed the four would travel together. They found two Indians willing to help them part of the way.

So now began what can only be described as weeks of slaving as Service was forced to exert himself more than he had ever done in his life. His canoe was placed in the scow which had to be rowed up the Peel to its junction with the Rat River. Then it was a case of rowing up the Rat until the narrowness of its headwaters forced them to forsake rowing for poling. As the river grew shallow they attached ropes to a home-made harness and adopted the role he described as being that of a yoke-ox and beaver with the working capacity of both. And so they slowly progressed, working twelve hours a day, up to their knees in water, plunging and panting, their eyes drawn to the hills ahead, continually seeking the easiest passage. At times they would run out of water, and their goods would have to be unloaded as they worked the scow on skids or runners over dry land: some days they only made a mile in twelve hours. Yet Service gives the impression that amidst all the toil and the apparent impossibility of the task he was in a strange way experiencing happiness. They had plenty to eat, the trappers saw to that, and having committed themselves, there could be no going back. He expressed his thoughts simply:

> We were launched on a bold adventure and the river was doing its best to balk us. The idea, it seemed to say, of trying to take a scow over the Rockies! It had never been done, never would be done – yet, as we strained upward a path opened for us. It's like Life, I thought banally. Difficulties daunt us, but if we tackle them with a high heart barriers break down and the way is clear.

But the Indians had now had enough, and they departed with obvious joy, leaving the the others to think that they had got out just before they were completely lost. But turning back was not an option for Service and his friends. On they strove, experiencing relief and joy when they encountered a channel that would take the scow; heartbreak when the water ran out and they were faced with manhandling the boat over miles of rough ground. And then one day the realisation came to them – they were no longer pulling the scow uphill but on the level, and in the far distance they could see the small lake which marked the height of the Divide. But the approaches to the lake were swampy and it took ten hours of wading and pulling, most of the time up to their waists in mud, before the clear waters of the lake were reached.

The party rested at the lake for a couple of days with Service working on his canoe to get it in peak condition for the rest of the trip. He had already indicated that when they reached the Bell

River he intended going forward on his own. And in due course this is what he did, fully realising that a minor accident like a sprain or losing his rifle or food in a canoe upset could have frightening consequences. But after some initial turbulence the Bell seemed to warrant the name he gave it of *la belle rivière*. Clear, placid, its banks abounding with ptarmigan, rabbits and hares, it transported him into an Arcadian world. The fish were so accommodating they seemed to jump straight from the river into his frying pan. For two hundred miles this beautiful river nurtured his whims as he drifted downstream with only an occasional touch of his blade required to correct his course. Then as the weather broke, he ran into the heavier current of the Porcupine.

The rest of the journey that was to take him to Dawson was not without incident. He met up again with Captain and Mrs McTosh and Jake Skilly, and because the two men were now at loggerheads agreed to take Skilly down to Dawson with him. Skilly was absolutely addicted to cigarette smoking, and as his supply of paper diminished he began to fear life without nicotine. He compelled Service to listen to ghastly tales about men in the wilds who had come to blows over apparently trivial matters and then would put a personal slant on the story, reminding Service how competent he was with an axe. Service became more and more concerned about his own safety as Skilly experienced and displayed withdrawal symptoms. It was with considerable relief he encountered a sternwheeler on the river and hoisting his canoe on board, booked his passage to Dawson. (Skilly was later to return to the Arctic to trap, and eventually shoot himself.) It was on this journey as the sternwheeler made its way up the Yukon river that Service composed his song, *When The Ice-Worm Nests Again*, so widely regarded as the song of the Yukon.

Service settled down quickly and quietly in Dawson. He shaved off his beard and returned to his bohemian lifestyle. He was magnificently fit and took daily ice baths, to keep himself physically hard. As Winter returned he put on snowshoes and rejoiced in his favourite exercise of beating trail through the woods.

He had the idea of a third book of verse using material from the basin of the Mackenzie and the Arctic. He developed his own method of revising his verse. He pinned the long rolls of paper used by paper-hangers to his cabin walls and printed his verse in large letters. Then he adjusted and changed his words and phrases until he had verse that looked right as well as sounded right. He took his time over his work feeling that there was no need to hurry. But there was to be one unasked for and unwanted adventure before his third book was completed.

Service set out one day on snow-shoes to visit friends who, he said, lived nigh on fifty miles from Dawson – a casual statement which hides a considerable physical feat. He stayed the night with them and set out to return to Dawson in the morning. Somehow on the return journey he lost his way, and the corrections he made to his line of travel were of no avail; he could not pick up a landmark he recognised. He trudged on hoping to find some indication of

Thousands visit this shrine of Service's today where readings of his verse are regularly given

his whereabouts, but ultimately as the skies darkened, he had to accept that he was lost.

From then on it was survival tactics. His walk became a stagger as he tired. The temperature dropped and he reckoned it was around forty-five below zero. Aware that he could not go on in case he walked into a snow drift and did not have the energy to get out, he made for some trees. His intention was to keep walking round the same tree all night and try to get his bearings in the morning. He selected a big pine and started his circular walk, growing more and more tired; he remembered feeling his number was just about up when the moon broke through with abnormal brilliance and there, not a hundred yards away, was a cabin.

Somehow he reached it – the law of the trail prevailed, it was unlocked and the stove was ready to be fired. He lit the stove and remembers having something to eat before he collapsed exhausted. However, the trauma was not yet over. The owner of the cabin arrived back in the morning, made sure Service was well fed, and easily prevailed on him to stay the next night to get his strength back. But that night the owner took to the whisky bottle, and in his cups, waving a loaded rifle at Service, revealed that he was the man known as Cannibal Joe, because some said he had killed and eaten his partner one winter when the two of them had run out of food on a trapping trip. In a tense atmosphere the trapper told his version of the story, how his partner had died and the dogs had eaten him; and he in turn had eaten the dogs. Service thrived on tales of the North, but the relief he felt when morning came and he was able to leave the cabin can be imagined.

Service worked through the winter on his third book and finished it as the first boat broke through the ice to reach the town. It was to be his last winter in the Yukon. One day a surprising and unexpected letter reached his cabin from the editor of the *Toronto Star*. Would he, asked the editor, care to report for the paper the rather obscure war which had broken out in the Balkans between Turkey and Bulgaria? 'With curses in my heart,' said Service, 'I cabled acceptance.' Thus, with a book of verse in his valise, in superb health, but uncouth through long living near to nature, he departed for sophisticated Europe. He was not to keep the promise he made to himself as the sternwheeler fumed into the current of the river, the promise to return to the land that had made him a legend. Instead, he was to leave a piece of his heart in a rickety old cabin:

> I hear the world-call and the clang of the fight;
> I hear the hoarse cry of my kind;
> Yet well do I know, as I quit you tonight,
> It's Youth that I'm leaving behind.
> And often I'll think of you, empty and black,
> Moose antlers nailed over your door;
> Oh, if I should perish my ghost will come back
> To dwell in you, cabin, once more!

Good-Bye, Little Cabin

CHAPTER 5

Characters of the Yukon

I hid all trace of her heart unclean;
I painted a babe at her breast;
I painted her as she might have been
If the Worst had been the Best.

My Madonna

SERVICE'S PLACE IN LITERATURE is examined later, but this is an appropriate place to pause and look at a prolific source of material for his Yukon verse – the women and men of the Yukon. Let us look at the ladies first. But not all the ladies of the Yukon – the overly-virtuous and the Nursing Sisters of St Anne, for example, did not figure in his work. Writers need colour, and it was to the dance hall girls and those who competed in a man's world that Service gave his attention. Many of them became legends even in their own lifetime. There was Klondike Kate who entertained the patrons of the Savoy Theatre, performing her flame dance attired in an expensive Paris gown with lighted candles on her head. It was said that her legs were always bruised from the nuggets thrown to her by admirers while she was dancing. There was Cad Wilson with a string of nuggets round the waist rousing the Sourdoughs to sing her song, *Such a Nice Girl Too*.

In 1975, the Yukon Status of Women Council published a book, *Yukon Women*, and was brave and broad-minded enough to comment on how these girls made their fortunes:

> ... a dance lasted a few moments and it cost a man a dollar. We girls received half for each dance; we got commission of twenty-five cents on each drink a partner bought, and a dollar on each bottle he purchased. Besides we were paid a salary of twenty dollars a week...

we thought nothing of paying twenty dollars for a pair of slippers to wear one or two nights, or as much as five hundred for an evening gown.

To say these were the women who inspired Service is not to suggest that he was a regular frequenter of dance halls. Deacons of the church seldom are. And indeed he would claim he did not swallow a drop of alcohol for the three years he spent in White-horse, and dance halls were hardly the haunts of teetotallers. Whether or not Service knew or even met any of the famous dance hall girls must remain a matter of conjecture. Although his poems suggest friendship he makes no mention of any of them in his memoirs. Besides, by the time he reached the Yukon the gold rush was on the decline, and the famous palaces of entertainment were closing down. But, empty or not, the dance halls were standing as living proof of what had been, and there would be no shortage of old-timers to fill his head with yarns about the girls.

In *I Married the Klondike*, Laura Berton points out that Dawson Society knew how to keep its distance from certain ladies:

I was at one concert in the A.B. Hall when three of these handsome and full-figured sirens, led by Sweet Marie, entered the place and brazenly (as all decent women agreed) seated themselves in an open box in the gallery. An undercurrent of excitement ran through the audience, but in a moment a Mountie appeared in the box, spoke a few words, and the women departed. Over these people - indeed over any who didn't behave - the Mounties held the threat of a blue ticket: an order to get out of town on the next boat.

But to Service, these ladies offered inspiration for his verse, and they brought a touch of homeliness to a male-dominated population. The Klondike would not have been the Klondike it was without their contribution to its wild night life. Service has made his contribution to those pages of frontier history.

Again, the Yukon Status of Women Council reminds us that

women shared the same privations as men in making their way to the Klondike, and had carried their loads up the White and Chilkoot Passes. With a view to developing businesses, many of their loads were unusual. Belinda Mulrooney made such a fortune from her hot water bottles she was able to buy a restaurant, the profits from which formed the basis for her expansion into a chain of roadhouses and mining development. Mrs Willis from her laundry profits could buy up mines which led her on to fortune. Less is known of the lady who carried loads of bread dough on her back, dough which rose with the heat of her body. These ladies fitted the words of the old song to perfection, they were indeed *Rough Tough Yukon Women*.

But it was to the ladies who operated and worked in the dance halls that Service's talents were drawn. The fact that in his advanced years he could still pen lines about them shows the impact they made on a level headed young man:

Fair ladies of my lusty youth,
I fear that you are dead and gone:
Where's Gertie of the diamond tooth,
Where's the Mare of Oregon?
What's become of Violet de Vere,
Claw-fingered Kate and Gumboot Sue?
They've crossed the Great Divide, I Fear;
Remembered now by just a few.

It is difficult to think of anyone failing to remember the 'Oregon Mare'. Ethel McNeil possessed the traditional 'kick like a mule', and any miner careless enough to pass an insulting remark within her hearing was liable to feel the strength of her footwork to the accompaniment of a neighing screech.

Although to the majority of his followers Service's most famous lady may be 'The lady that's known as Lou,' in fact we learn little about her, although obviously she is the source of the conflict in his poem of Dan McGrew. Lou is central to the story, but apart from her propensity to paint her face and relieve a dying man of his money, we know little about her. However there are two ladies of the dance halls who appear to have had a special appeal to Service. The first, because of her humour, is Violet de Vere.

Violet de Vere was a good looker. As Service said, 'Her sitting base out-faired the face of any girl in town.' Violet, though, appeared to have the ability to create disturbances, and on one occasion when being arrested, deemed it fitting behaviour for a lady to assault her apprehenders. In due course she appeared before the bench. After the judge had remonstrated with her over her actions he imposed a twenty dollar fine. The story of Violet's reaction has a delightful ending:

> 'I'm grateful to the court because I'm not put in the clink;
> There's twenty bucks to pay my fine – but now I come to think:
> Judge darlin', You've been owin' me five bucks for near a year;
> Take fifteen – there! We'll call it square', said Violet de Vere.

But the dance hall girl who claims Service's affection most strongly is Montreal Maree. Frequently mentioned *en passant*, three lengthy narratives about her are included in his verse. In all three there is a goodness to be told about.

In the poem of her name where 'Belchin Billy', likewise known as 'Windy Bill' is seeking gun in hand to shoot a competitor lover, who, unknown to him is hiding under her petticoats, the lines display her character:

> But of straight shootin' Dawson dames Maree was rated Queen,
> As pretty as a pansy, wi' a heart of hunker gold.

and again:

> I've heard it said that she got wed and made a wonder wife,
> I guess she did; that careless kid had mother in her heart.

In 'McClusky's Nell', McClusky is being entertained in a back room of the Nugget Bar by Violet de Vere, while his motherless child Nell is pathetically trying to find his whereabouts. Maree expresses fury at Violet de Vere depriving the child of her father's company, and the motley collection who make up the clientele of The Nugget gather round Nell and ask her to sing. Her rendering of a hymn tune so tears them apart that the Sourdoughs decide she must be sent outwith the Yukon to be brought up free from the vices of a mining camp. The miners give the money, and by the end of the poem little Nell has gone on to become a famous opera star.

Service, probably because of his vagabond years, was aware that social status and morality have but a tenuous relationship. Good and bad can be found in all places, and much depends on the perception of the viewer. 'My Madonna', where an artist paints a woman of the streets to be seen by another interpreter later as a biblical figure, makes the point strongly. In the dance hall girls, Service sees no grounds for sermonising. They were there, they displayed grit and courage, they added to the story of the Yukon. He will not cast the first stone against them.

When, however, we turn to the men of the Yukon as source material for Service's verse, the position is not so clear cut. The lives of Service's male characters have not been authenticated to anything like the same extent as the lives of the ladies. That Klondike Kate and the other dance hall girls mentioned above existed is not in doubt. Their activities have been researched and documented by many writers. But Barb-wire Bill, named after the 'brand of hooch to which he was most inclined', One-Eyed Mike, Pious Pete, Blasphemous Bill and so on are not found in either the history or the popular literature of the Yukon in the same way. This is not to suggest that such people did not exist, but the tales Service told of them seem to have been grafted on by Service himself to the characters he knew or heard of. And we have in addition to contend with the two vibrant characters who dominate all the others and who combine myth and fiction with fact. Sam MacGee, a respectable customer of Service's bank, had no link with the tale told about him. Dan

Some of the ladies who added colour to the Klondike scene

MacGrew might have been based on Soapy Smith, the killer who ruled Skagway just prior to Service's arrival in the north, but equally could have been inspired by any wild west tale. Service approached his Yukon men and women from different angles. The women were described as they were. The men developed as characters because of the tales he told about them.

But a greater difference in his use of men and women as source material is the more generalised approach used with the men. He sees the Klondike as a magnet which attracted a certain type of man, the restless, the wanderer, the sort who thought they might find their true niche in the Yukon, those who could not resist the call of the wild. Nowhere is the pain and confusion associated with the indescribable pull that forces men into taking the trail for far-off places more poignantly set out than in the *The Lure of Little Voices*.

> There's a cry from out the Loneliness – Oh, listen, Honey, listen!,
> Do you hear it, do you fear it, you're a-holding of me so?
> You're a sobbing in your sleep, dear, and your lashes, how they glisten –
> Do you hear the little Voices all a-beggin me to go?
> All a-begging me to leave you. Day and night they're pleading, praying,
> On the North wind, on the West wind, from the peak and from the plain,
> Night and day they never leave me – do you know what they are saying?
> 'He was ours before you got him, and we want him once again.'

Service surely was able to write with such feeling because he was cast in the restless mould himself. His Yukon verse is so powerful because in the Yukon he was able to achieve what he wanted from life at that time. In the men and women of the Yukon he saw kindred spirits. To him, the fact that so few struck it rich did not imply failure. Amidst the uncouthness of the Klondike and the silence of the Yukon many had found what they were looking for and that was not necessarily the richness of gold. That, he could and would write about:

> Now I've had my lazy supper, and the level sun is gleaming
> On the water where the silver salmon play;
> And I light my little corn-cob, and I linger softly dreaming,
> In the twilight of the land that's far away.
> I am one of you no longer: by the trails my feet have broken,
> The dizzy peaks I've scaled, the camp fire's glow,
> By the lonely seas I've sailed in – yea, the final word is spoken,
> I am signed and sealed to nature. Be it so.

CHAPTER 6

War Correspondent

Here is my Garret up five flights of stairs;
Here's where I deal in dreams and ply my fancies
Here is the wonder-shop of all my wares,
My sounding sonnets and my red romances.

My Garret

AFTER NINE YEARS IN THE High North it might be expected that a movement into an alien world of crowds and cosmopolitan incident would result in Service appearing startled and timid, perhaps even gauche. But nothing in the opening pages of *Harper of Heaven*, his second volume of autobiography, suggests he was in any way ill-at-ease in his new role of war correspondent. Like an actor playing a part, he is in no time sporting a fez and smoking the appropriate cigarettes. The observer in him was suited to cafe life; the people he encountered became characters; behind the trivial happenings of everyday life he saw stories worth telling.

Service had crossed the Atlantic on a German luxury liner where the arrogance of the ship's officers and most of the passengers had rankled with him. By way of Naples he reached Istanbul and, although kitted out in khaki and eager to see action, could not, like the other correspondents, get permission to go to the front. For a while idleness contented him; then he joined the Turkish Red Crescent with the hope of getting nearer to good copy for his paper. A spell working in a cholera camp swiftly reduced his enthusiasm for such work. He returned to Istanbul where he incurred the wrath of officialdom who had seen through his ploy. He was ordered to report to the police. Remembering that discretion is sometimes the better part of valour he decided against getting into further hot water. At the time of his appointment with the authorities he was being sick over the rail of a Rumanian steamer crossing the Black sea.

One is tempted to liken the next six months or so of Service's life to his vagabond days in America, although this time, of course, he had the safety net of a solid bank account. Bucharest was his first stopping place and his enthusiasm for it was still clear many years later.

> Bucharest thrilled me. I wrote bright articles of army officers in Merry Widow uniforms, of gargantuan coachmen driving their teams like the wind, of gay incongruities where East meets West and crude peasants gaze at the debonair boulevards.

On his way to that capital city he had travelled on the Orient Express, meeting a flamboyant aristocrat owning the proud name of Sir Pelham Pelham. Sir Pelham, who enjoyed the company of ladies, took Service under his wing for a while and later, as we shall see, almost embroiled him in a dangerous escapade of the heart.

From Bucharest, Service moved on to Budapest where, living in shabby accommodation, he, to use his phrase, 'glutted his hunger for obscurity.' Vienna was his next stopping place. A taxi-driver, not understanding his request for a modest base, took him to one of the city's grand hotels where in the foyer the first person he met was Sir Pelham Pelham. They dined together, much of the conversation centring around a Spanish countess whose beauty was having an effect on the noble knight's pulse rate. In *Harper of Heaven*, Service beautifully sets the scene.

> 'Well, she is an elegant eyeful,' I admitted. 'But, of course you know her?' 'Unfortunately no. I do not believe the lady understands English. However, in the language of love do we not all speak Esparanto?'
>
> 'Good gracious! You're not thinking of making love to her?'

'My love-making days are not over,' said Sir Pelham proudly.

I looked at him with admiration. What a buck he must have been at his best! 'Well, if you can't be good be careful,' I said. 'Don't go biting the Spanish Countess on the neck.'

He adjusted his monocle and gave me a cool stare. 'Will you bet me ten pounds I won't bite the Spanish Countess on the neck?'

'I wouldn't be a party to such an outrage.'

'Don't worry about the outrage part, that's my affair. Will you wager I won't bite the Castillian Countess on the neck?'

'I'll take you,' I said reluctantly.

Sir Pelham was willing to tread where angels feared. In due course he bit the neck of a surprised but delighted Countess as she was seated at a writing table. Sir Pelham had planned to claim that he was trying to remove a wasp, which had just stung her, from the shoulders of the Countess. He was not given the opportunity. The lady threw herself into his arms, declaring she knew by the way he had been looking at her that he was infatuated by her; that she had been waiting for something unexpected to happen.

However, as their passions subsided there was a realisation that the tooth marks would take some explaining to the lady's husband who was due to rejoin his wife the next day. There was talk about preparing for a duel with an irate husband. Thanks to the subterfuge of the Countess a way out was found. But Service had had enough of Sir Pelham and his ilk. Now was time to make for his golden goal of Paris.

Service arrived in Paris in the Spring of 1912. It was love at first sight. He intended staying two months; he remained, or had a base in the city, for fifteen years. His first day in Paris he claimed to be the most delectable day of his life: 'To be young, free, primed with romance and with a full purse – what could be nearer Paradise than Paris in the Spring?'

In Paris, the Bohemian in him came to the fore and stayed there. He moved into modest rooms on the Quai Voltaire where, sitting at his window, he could watch the activities on the Seine. He attended art classes. Most important of all, he moved in the company of the prominent international correspondents, journalists and writers, poets, novelists and humorists who, either permanently or in transience, were gracing the literary scene in Paris at that time.

He struck up a friendship with Neil Munro. Some, like Richard Harding Davis, he revered from a distance, while with Edmund Gosse he was not afraid to return repartee. He could not change from being able to write only to please himself, but nevertheless Paris made his feelings more tender, and brought a delightful whimsy into his verse:

Now, it was in the month of May
As wrestling with a rhyme rheumatic,
I chanced to look across the way,
And, lo! within a neighbour attic,
A hand drew back the window shade,
And there, a picture glad and glowing,
I saw a sweet and slender maid,
And she was sewing, sewing, sewing.

God love her! how it cheered me then
To see her there so brave and pretty;
So she with needle, I with pen,
We slaved and sang above the city.
And as across my streams of ink
I watched her from a poet's distance,
She stitched and sang – I scarely think
She was aware of my existence.

In *Ballads of a Bohemian*, his collection of verse about his Paris days, Service intersperses his verse with paragraphs about his life-style, about various events and his philosophy at that time. At least it cannot be argued that he did not practise what he preached.

> I awoke this morning to see the bright sunshine flooding into my garret. No chamber in the palace of a king could have been more fair. How I sang as I dressed! How I lingered over my coffee, savouring every drop! How carefully I packed my pipe, gazing serenely over the rooves of Paris.

> ... Yet I think I shall always remain a Bohemian. I hate regularity. The clock was never made for me. I want to eat when I am hungry, sleep when I am weary, drink – well, any old time.

> I prefer to be alone. Company is a constraint to my spirit. I never make an appointment if I can avoid it. To do so is to put a mortgage on my future. I like to be able to rise in the morning with the thought that the hours before me are all mine, to spend in my own way – to work, to dream, to watch the unfolding drama of life.

Being the possessor of a sturdy pair of legs, Service used them to tramp the length and breadth of the city. But it was inevitable that the time would come when an inner urge would compel him to search further afield. He bought a bicycle and started to explore. He first explored Normandy and then moved on to Brittany. Like so many Scots who respond to the Celtic influence that pervades the land of the Breton, he was enchanted by all he saw. He wrote about the fishermen and their lives, spent hours exploring its beaches and islets and once again drew close to nature. Then one day he saw, to use his own words, 'a little cottage for sale that seemed to cry out for me to buy it.' Without crossing its portal, he made the purchase, and returned to Paris. He wanted, he said, 'to keep it a dream, something insubstantial and only half conceived.'

In his autobiography, Service refers to his cottage, which he

'Dream Haven'. For over forty years this was the house that held his heart.

had now named Dream Haven, as a little red-roofed house. Small, though, it is not.

A former coast-guard station, it stands within substantial policies in a commanding position on a rocky promontory overlooking a bay dotted with islands. And anyone familiar with Brittany would be surprised at the description of it as being 'red-roofed'. The houses in this land of Celtic connections are grey-roofed without apparent exception. But for some inexplicable reason Dream Haven did have a red roof when Service bought it, and it was always a point of regret with him that when it had to be re-roofed he was unable to find suitable tiles the colour of the originals. Dream Haven now conforms to local custom with a grey roof.

However, now being the possessor of a house, with a practical turn of mind, he started to think about matrimony. He knew that the Latin Quarter was unlikely to produce the kind of lifemate who would satisfy his inner need for a respectable and thrifty wife. The free and easy life of the Latin Quarter was a spur to writing, but it was at variance with the presbyterian values that still held sway over the inner man. So, everything had to be left to chance, or Providence, and once again he was to be cared for by his lucky star.

Within three months he was married to a distiller's daughter he met by sheer chance in the street while watching a procession. She married him believing him to be a penniless writer; she was only to discover Dream Haven later on a trip to Brittany. Their marriage was to be a long and happy one.

The newly-weds moved into an apartment on the Boulevard Montparnasse where Service settled down to write a novel about the Latin Quarter, paying little attention to the stirrings of conflict in Europe. He finished his book *The Pretender*, within six months. Its opening sentence: 'To have omnibus tastes and an automobile income – how ironic?' indicates there is a measure of autobiographical material worked into the novel.

The Pretender is not the kind of book people would rush out to buy today. Told in the first person, its plot is good but the structure of the story cumbersome. Service wrote about things familiar to him, so there is realism in the book but it lacks the speed and flow that would take it to great heights. In many ways it is what is to be expected from a second novel.

A first book writes itself, the author perhaps having lived with its theme for years. The second is a hard job of work and one suspects Service worked too hard at trying to include everything that would make it a success.

But if it failed with the reading public, Service remained true to it. It was always his favourite among the novels he wrote. 'Perhaps,' he said, 'because I was so radiant when I wrote it.' Perhaps, one may add, because there was so much of himself in it.

The Services were now sharing their time between Paris and Brittany. And though he was long to remain true to Paris, there were occasions when the urge for a return to the simple life could not be restrained. In *Ballads of a Bohemian*, he wrote:

The Café De La Paix,

August 1, 1914.

Paris and I are out of tune. As I sit at this famous corner the faint breeze is stale and weary; stale and weary too, the faces that swirl around me; while overhead the electric sign of Somebody's Chocolate appears and vanishes with irritating insistency. The very trees seem artificial, gleaming under the arc-lights with a raw virility that rasps my nerves.

'Poor little trees,' I mutter, 'growing in all this grime and glare.' –

– 'Tell me, O wistful trees, what shall I do?' Then that stale and weary wind rustles the leaves of the nearest sycamore, and I am sure it whispers: 'Brittany.'

So tomorrow I am off, off to the Land of Little Fields.

Oh, I will go to Finistèrre, there's nothing that can hold me back.
I'll laugh with Yves and Léon, and I'll chaff with Rose and Jeanne;
I'll seek the little, quaint buvette that's kept by Mother Merdrinac,
Who wears a cap of many frills, and swears just like a man.
I'll yarn with hearty, hairy chaps who dance and leap and crack their heels;
Who swallow cupfuls of cognac and never turn a hair;
I'll watch the nut-brown boats come in with mullet, plaice and conger eels.
The jewelled harvest of the sea they reap in Finistèrre.

But the idyllic life in Brittany Service enjoyed in that Summer of 1914 was not to last. Returning from a walk one afternoon he heard the village clock peal, its ring taken up in sombre chorus by bells all over the countryside. He knew what it meant. He made for the village square in time to hear the *Garde Champêtre* read the mobilisation announcement. In later years he would pay for the building of the village war memorial in that self-same square. In a state of indecision, the Services returned to Paris.

CHAPTER 7

Paris and the War

That poilu across the way,
With the shrapnel wound in his head,
Has a sister: she came today
To sit awhile by his bed.
All morning I heard him fret:
"Oh, when will she come, Fleurette?"

Fleurette

FOR SOMEONE OF SERVICE'S apparent health and vitality, it must
have come as something of a shock to be turned down as unfit to
go to war. He had darkened his hair and understated his years in
an attempt to conceal the fact that he was over the accepted age
for combat. The Seaforth Highlanders was the regiment of his
choice, but a varicose vein let him down; a blemish he should have
been grateful for, as the Seaforths were almost wiped out at one of
the early battles of the Somme. Remaining true to the assessment
he had of himself, he had rejected the advice given to him by his
brilliant friend John Buchan to try for a commission. It was in the
ranks as an ordinary soldier, removed from the making of life and
death decisions, that he felt his contribution lay. With that door
closed he turned elsewhere.

Remembering his Balkan experiences, he made application to
his old newspaper syndicate, and was once again accredited as a war
correspondent. To those with memories of the Second World War,
the term 'War Correspondent' may hold a certain amount of glamour. It was not ever thus; in the early years of the First World War
the military hierarchy had a positive dislike, if not hatred, of journalists who took too great an interest in the running of the war. Such

people had to be kept in their place, and their place did not include free access to the front or the main hives of military activity. It was not long, then, before Service found himself in Calais, in the company of many other correspondents dependent on the information, duly censored and double checked, given to them by authority.

This was not to Service's liking, and realising that Dunkirk offered a greater insight into troop and war material movements, he decided to make for the port. Dunkirk however was a place forbidden to correspondents. Service's answer was to take the train to the station before Dunkirk and walk the rest of the way. Once there he was able to watch the arrival of supply columns from England, note the condition of German prisoners being herded into prisoner-of-war camps, and speak to wounded Tommies on their way to 'Blighty'.

But for once his luck did not hold; in a place consumed with spy fever his actions were noticed by an alert gendarme. He was arrested and confined in a small white-washed cell. His linguistic ability and the admission that he had illegally entered the town added weight to the police view that his papers were irregular and that he was a spy. The seriousness of his situation in a 'shoot first and ask questions afterwards' atmosphere was not lost on him. It was only at a later stage of his interrogation when a British officer joined his inquisitors that his story was accepted. With a reprimand stinging in his ears, he returned to Paris, still determined to get into the war.

Service found Paris in a state of chaos. Such had been the force and speed of the German advance that many expected German troops would be marching up the Champs Elysees within a few weeks. Service continued to send off reports to his paper, but one day he saw an advertisement which caught his interest: it referred to the formation of an American Ambulance Unit which was looking for drivers for front-line duties. He went for an interview, where he discovered it was rather an upper-crust unit made up of car owners prepared to convert their vehicles into ambulances. On the understanding that he did not write about what he saw (a condition he had mental reservations about), he was accepted into the corps. Given the status of gentleman-driver he was entitled to wear an officer-type uniform. An early note from the front perhaps suggests a slightly dashing approach to his new war job.

The Somme Front,

January 1915

... There is an avenue of noble beeches leading to the Chateau, and in the shadow of each glimmers the pale oblong of an ambulance. We have to keep them thus concealed, for only yesterday morning a Taube flew over. The beggars are rather partial to Red Cross cars. One of our chaps, taking in a load of wounded, was chased and pelted the other day.

The Chateau seems all spires and towers, the glorified dream of a Parisian pastrycook. On its terrace figures in khaki are lounging. They are the volunteers, the owner drivers of the Corps, many of them men of wealth and title. Curious to see one who owns all the coal in two counties proudly signing for his sou a day; or another, who lives in a Fifth Avenue palace, contentedly sleeping on the straw-strewn floor of a hovel.

Here is a rhyme I have made of such a one:

Jerry MacMullen the millionaire,
Driving a red-meat bus out there-
How did he win his Croix de Guerre?
Bless you, that's old stuff:
Beast of a night on the Verdun road,
Jerry struck with a woeful load,
Stalled in the mud where the red lights glowed,
Prospect devilish tough.

A month later it is straight reporting as he writes:

Running the car into the shadow of a ruined house, I try to sleep. But a battery starts to blaze away close by and the flame lights up my shelter. Near me some soldiers are in deep slumber; one stirs in his sleep as a big rat runs over him, and I know by experience that when one is sleeping a rat feels as heavy as a sheep.

But how can one possibly sleep? Out there in the dark there is the wild tattoo of a thousand rifles, and hark! that dull roar is the explosion of a mine. Desperate things are doing. There will be lots of work for me before this night is over. What a cursed place!

And later, the awfulness of the war comes through.

Ah! I was never intended for a job like this. I realise it more and more every day, but I will stick it out till I break down. To be nervous, over-imaginative, terribly sensitive to suffering, is a poor equipment for the man who starts out to drive wounded on the battlefield. I am haunted by the thought my car may break down when I have a load of wounded. Once indeed it did and many died while I waited for help. Now I never look at what is given me. It might unnerve me.'

Whatever his fears he did not crack: he undertook what was required of him – outpost duty, collecting the wounded in no-man's land. He survived Champagne and Verdun. The entry under his name in the *Canadian Who's Who* says he was decorated three times although it does not stipulate what these awards were. Then, his health giving way, he returned to Dream Haven. The experiences of war were fresh in his mind and as his health returned so he started to put his memories into words – the result was his *Rhymes of a Red Cross Man* which he dedicated to his brother who had been killed in action serving with the Canadian forces. The success of this book especially in America, was phenomenal: for nine months it headed the list of best-sellers in *The Bookman*.

Service's return to health coincided with America's entry into the war. The Ambulance Corps was disbanded. As he said, 'All those young folk who talked with an American accent and wore handkerchiefs in their sleeves had joined the regulars.' It was time to find another war job.

That there are such things as good war jobs cannot be denied. And now Service was to be given a plum. He was asked by the Canadian Government to report on the activities of the Canadian Expeditionary Force. This was an unrestricted appointment, and, provided with a guide and chauffeur, he was to visit Canadian troops both in the front line and in their back-up operations. It was a job to which he was most admirably suited. From battlefield to lumber camps he moved, recording the Canadian contribution to the war. He met with former cronies, and in a never-to-be-forgotten moment became the first person to enter Lille after the German troops had retreated.

It is just as well he had an occupation which demanded his full attention at that time, because in his private life he had been dealt the most hurtful of blows.

In 1917 Service had become the proud father of twin girls, Doris and Iris. 'Proud', in his case, seems to have been an understatement. He was absolutely over the moon with joy. A year later while in Menton, Doris contracted scarlet fever from which she died. Service was shattered.

Writing to a friend some six months later, this figure of the battlefield would confess he still could not think about his loss without breaking down. A poem he wrote to mark the event, and which was never published, finishes with the saddest lines he would ever write:

My little girl, whose smile so bright,
I'll see while sight endures!
This life of mine I'd give tonight
Could I but ransom yours.

Then one morning in Paris a few months later as he was typing his dispatches he heard the bells ring out the tidings that the war was over. For a while he shared the euphoria of those in the

A very military looking Robert Service towards the end of the First World War

streets, then, realising that the mirth-mad crowd were not dropping tears for those who had died, he gathered his chattels together for a return to Dream Haven.

Thus far in Service's life there had been a regular thirst for adventure, or at least for exploring the unusual. But the war years had slaked that thirst, and especially over the next two years one senses a change in the man. The retreat into the shell of his family became more obvious, and unexpectedly and surprisingly there are signs of a somewhat lofty attitude being adopted. The purchase of his magnificent residence in the Place du Pantheon and the unnecessary wearing of a monocle were perhaps manifestations of this. His comment in *Harper of Heaven* that, 'in these days, I refused to write to anyone,' is more telling. Was this shielding of himself an advance warning of the barriers he would later build between himself and the world? Or was this behaviour just his response to the war as he moved to a more conventional life-style, allowing the pendulum to swing that little bit extra in its arc.

He had, of course, the assurance of a man with no financial worries. Indeed, for a time it seemed that, try as he might, his expenditure in no way kept up with an ever-increasing income. His investments rose. And in this carefree environment his interest in the finer things of life burst through. The fruits of his reading of the finest writers over the years were now to be harvested.

What had been hidden before was now obvious for all to see: he had become a man of culture. And the after-war years were exciting years for those with such interests. Although not a front player in the scene, he was part of it. How else could he have written:

> Blocking the doorway of Sylvia Beach's bookshop one could see the portly form of Ford Maddox Ford accompanied by the vivacious Violet Hunt. In the shop with its Shakespearian sign one would run into James Joyce peering shortsightedly at the shelves, or Antheil the composer, buzzing with enthusiasm. In the Quarter were many who afterwards became famous – Giants in Gestation.

Service, though, had his own contribution to make to the literary scene. He was working on his *Ballads of Bohemian*, which deals in turn with the Latin Quarter, Brittany and the War. He wrote, 'Because it was the most autobiographical of all my verse books I dislike it the least.' Yet his followers were fickle and it was not to achieve the sales of his other books of verse. Read as pure autobiography it is a splendid book with much high quality verse. Different certainly from his Yukon lines, there is a soundness and maturity in it which makes it ideal armchair reading. He is no longer just the writer of 'good newspaper verse.'

> For all of worth that in this clay abides,
> The leaping rapture and the ardent flame,
> The hope, the high resolve, the faith that guides;
> All is Thine, and liveth in Thy name:
> Lord, have I dallied with the sacred fire!
> Lord, have I trailed Thy glory in the Mire!

But Service's revulsion from the war was now over. The urge for new sights was once again stirring. The catalyst was the news that one of his books was to be made into a film. 'Buy a big steamer trunk and pack it,' was his order one day to his family – 'We're going to Hollywood.'

CHAPTER 8

Hollywood and Tahiti

'Flowers, only flowers – bring me dainty posies,
Blossoms for forgetfulness,' that was all he said.

IN THE NINETEEN TWENTIES, it was a long haul from Paris to Los Angeles. The steamer that carried Service, his wife and daughter to New York was crammed to capacity and it was a relief to disembark, even if New York did not capture their hearts. As the train sped westwards, we can imagine Service having thoughts about his earlier time in California when he was short of both money and prospects. But on the family arrival in the Golden State he had to contend with changes. The old frame building which had provided his previous lodgings for two 'bits' a night had been ousted by a skyscraper and the orange groves where he had toiled were now replaced by factories. And, of course, the term 'Hollywood' now meant more than the name of a suburb of Los Angeles.

Service was fascinated by the film-making capital of the world. Just seeing figures such as Charlie Chaplin and Noah Beery was exciting. He interviewed Louis Mayer: 'He was dapper and affable and spent an hour with me,' reported Service, 'I still have a picture of us arm in arm, but today he is as unapproachable as Royalty itself.'

Service invited his mother down from Alberta to meet his family. His mother and wife took an instant liking to each other, and as they grew in companionship an idea which had been with Service for some time could not be held back further. Choosing an appropriate moment, he announced, no doubt with some apprehension, that he would like to go to the South Seas to gather material for a novel. His mother's reply shows to what extent she had been incorporated into his family life. 'By all means go, Willie,' she said, using his family name 'and write your book.' 'Oh, these men,' she added in an aside, 'they give me a pain in the neck – they think they're so darned indispensable.'

Within three days he was bound for Tahiti.

While no doubt Service's ambition to go to the South Seas was prompted by his desire to write a novel, he was also to admit that he was once again feeling the call of the open road, the need for adventure. He had long been fascinated by the South Seas – Stevenson had seen to that. And Somerset Maugham, who would later become a near neighbour on the Riviera, with his *Moon and Sixpence*, was proving that stories set in the area had wide appeal.

Service loved the indolence and tranquility of Tahiti

Tahiti lies some three and a half thousand miles to the south-west of California. Its beauty is legendary. Well wooded mountains with numerous cascades provide the perfect backdrop to the fertile lowlands with their abundance of coconuts and oranges and the easily grown breadfruit, yams and sweet potatoes. Cook, when he visited the islands in 1769, had given the coral-encircled archipelago the name of The Society Islands in honour of the Royal Society of London, a name which did not find favour with the French who were later to turn this garden of the Pacific into one of their colonies.

Service landed at Tahiti's capital Papeete, and quickly succumbed to the indolence and tranquillity of the place. He rented a bungalow, finding it easy to spend much of the day lolling in a hammock. There were two hotels in Papeete and he gave them his custom on alternate days. There was little to choose between them; 'Both,' he claimed, 'provided the same tough chicken and the same number of ants in the soup.' But it comes as no surprise that he quickly sickened of the torpid life, and castigated himself for the expansion of his waistline. Inevitably he felt the need to stretch his legs and made the decision to walk round Tahiti, living rough, and dependent on the fruits of nature for his sustenance.

Thus he came to know the people of the island and respect their natural kindness and courtesy as they provided him with a mat in their houses for the night, or shared the meal they had prepared for him, after spying him from a distance making for their home. And when a house was not at hand for the night, Service would make a little bower for himself between the large surface roots of the trees. Deprived of a razor, he took on an unkempt appearance, but that did not seem to frighten the young people:

... On a fallen tree a boy was whittling, and the shadow of the leaves made a pattern on his bare brown back. There on a grassy point, shaded by palms, was the village...

By tiny huts of thatch and bamboo were heaps of unhusked nuts. In sheds hung bunches of amber feis, and through a hedge of crimson catspaw I saw a golden baby, eating a mango. He stared at me with big black eyes, his fat face obscured by the yellow globe. Then suddenly he howled with a mouth full of mango, but the whittling boy went to comfort him. He brought two magnificent mangoes and

> with a bow presented them to me. It was done with the grace of a
> Spanish grandee. What a lovable people and how happy they were.

At the end of a week Service returned to his bungalow, enjoying again the experience of being clean and clad in white ducks. A retired soldier he had become friendly with, offered him hospitality on a neighbouring island where he owned a plantation. This provided the thrill of beaching from a raging surf. Later he would express the opinion that if he had to labour for his keep, the tending of vanilla vines was the most acceptable face that work could wear. But wherever he travelled, his notebook was at the ready, recording material for the novel he would later write under the title of *The Roughneck*. But until he returned to the bosom of his family it was to be rum punch and roast pig and paunchiness. He succumbed to the world of the Lotus Eater.

Carl F. Klinck who has analysed Service's novels probably more than any other writer, makes the point that had Service concentrated on being a travel writer, he might have rivalled the authors he had so recently read. It is a most valid point. Many of the descriptions Service provides in *The Roughneck* and in *Harper of Heaven* are indeed splendid, the reader seeming to be at one with the islanders and the islands. It is as an observer and reporter, whether in verse or prose, that Service is supreme. The plot in *The Roughneck* is rather too involved. But the story moves with a good flow; the stiltedness of his earlier books has gone. And his bad men are really bad:

> The beach of Papeete was like a sink in which were deposited the
> dregs and scourings of the Seven Seas. The elite of Papeete black-
> guardism was the gang of Bad Marc Macara.

> It was said he would admit none but those who had been in prison
> or had killed their man. All qualified as far as the first condition was
> concerned; several admitted to the second.

Macara had an ambition. He wanted to be a king, the despotic ruler of some island remote and savage. One of the Solomons, for instance. He would subdue the local tribe, debauch the women, enslave the men. By terror and cruelty he would dominate them, so that in time he would reign like a real king, surrounded by a harem of black Marys and sustained by unlimited rum. His followers would share in his prosperity, and, once they were firmly established, would live on the fat of the land.

In due course, *The Roughneck* was to be made into a film with George O'Brien in the starring role. Its success added to the Service coffers.

But Service had not quite finished with the South Seas. Later on in his song *Raratonga* he was to indicate that his Tahiti sojourn had been one happy caper:

Oh I'm going back to Raratonga, I'm sick of all society and swank;
I wouldn't linger here a moment longer, If you gave me all the
    money in the bank;
I know the boys will welcome me out yonder, And the girlies will be
    laughing as I land,
So I'm off, I'm off to Raratonga, With my little ukulele in my hand.
No bills for board I'll pay in Raratonga, I'll pick the blushing bread
    fruit from the tree;
And if perhaps my appetite be stronger, I'll flick a ruddy lobster from
    the sea;
No tailor duns I'll have in Raratonga, Of two banana leaves I'll make
    a kilt,
And a dusky belle will wriggle like a conger, And dance the hu-la-
    hu-la to this lilt.

Back in Hollywood, Service helped his mother prepare to return to Canada. Her diversions were cards and reading mystery stories, and Service was continually under pressure from her to write a detective novel. Shortly after her departure the Services were on their way back to Paris. Perhaps 'returning home' would be a better expression, because, without his books and paintings Service never felt truly at home anywhere. And so he settled down for a while to what might be called a normal existence, enjoying the precious years when there was delight in taking his daughter to school and later listening to her tales of the day's happenings. But as we have seen, with Service there always had to be some adventure in the offing, be it a journey or just a new experience. The catalyst for his next venture, which was to bring him close to the world of the *apache*, was his mother's insistence he write a gangster story to satisfy her craving for such tales. He started to explore the slums of Paris getting to know the lower depths, he claimed, better than any other British writer:

> The rue Mouffetard is a steep, unsavoury street that seethes with sordid humanity. The houses are mouldering with age, the doors dark tunnels burrowing into decrepitude. In an evil half-light sinister shadows haunt it. Every second entry is a bar and in its dim depths men with faces entirely evil foregather. Near it is the rue St. Medard, frequented by the garbage-rakers and close by the Flea Market, where they sell their finds. Round the Place Maubert radiate poisonous alleys and close by is the Cafe des Clochards, refuge of those homeless outcasts who sleep under the bridges of the Seine.
>
> In this furtive region, by day and by night, I prowled, wearing a turtle-necked sweater, a cloth cap and old flannel trousers. Thus disguised it was quite a trick to get away from my swank apartment without shocking the other tenants; but I was aided by my concierge, an ex-policeman, who understood my motive. He entered into my slumming activities, so that I slipped off my raincoat and slunk out without anyone recognising the tough looking bum as the monocled individual who stared arrogantly at them in the elevator.

As Service explored the sweaty parlours he saw scenes of the utmost depravity. Huddled in the corner of a cafe or dance hall, he took in the world of pimps and prostitutes, deviationists and addicts, watched the behaviour of the brutal apache, their treatment of their women and their willingness to draw knives and fight amongst themselves. The music of the dens fascinated him, the chaloupe and the tango especially, where the forcefulness of the music could arouse a fury within the dancers.

His book did not lack colour or characters; he took himself off to Brittany and finished it within nine months. It became a best seller. Yet, good as it was, one still feels that his verse was better than his prose; that his rhymes hold the reader closer than his sentences:

> You've heard of Julot the apache, and Gigolette, his môme–
> Montmartre was their hunting ground, but Belville was their home.
> A little chap just like a boy, with smudgy black moustache,-
> Yet there was nothing juvenile in Julot the apache.
> From head to heel as tough as steel, as nimble as a cat,
> With every trick of twist and kick, a master of savate.
> And Gigolette was tall and fair, as stupid as a cow,
> With three combs in the greasy hair she banged upon her brow.
> You'd see her on the Place Pigalle on any afternoon,
> A primitive and strapping wench as brazen as the moon.
> And yet there is a tale that's told of Clichy after dark,
> And two gendarmes who swung their arms with Julot for a mark.
> And oh, but they'd have got him too, they banged and blazed away,
> When like a flash a woman leapt between them and their prey.
> She took the medicine meant for him; she came down with a crash–
> 'Quick now, and make you getaway, O Julot the apache-'

In *Harper of Heaven*, there is a ten year period between the nineteen twenties and thirties when Service has little to say about the production of his verse and prose. Writing to a friend in Canada in the early twenties he indicates both his firm family attachment and then a certain restlessness:

> I am at my place by the sea, and intend remaining until nearly
> Christmas. I shall be all alone which is necessary for my work and am

sending the family to Paris. Iris is now quite a little girl and doing very well indeed. She was inclined to be delicate but seems to have quite grown out of it.

... I don't write with much enthusiasm these days. Getting old, I suppose; and then I have enough money to live on nicely without working. However, if I gave up entirely I should be bored, as I cannot develop any hobbies. I like motoring. Tennis is too strenuous, and golf too difficult. I think I will take up trout fishing as a gentle pastime for my declining years. On the side hills of the Alps they tell me there are good streams. I do not think I will ever again visit Canada When I think of Dawson and all that life it seems like a dream. I used to consider myself a bit of an authority on the Yukon, but now my ignorance is abysmal.

Of course, one reason for the seeming lack of importance that writing had in his life at this time was the fact that he had a health problem. A passionate believer in fitness, he forgot that fitness is related to age, a point his doctor had to make when he sought clearance to enter a boxing tournament at the age of fifty. Robust in health with rippling muscles he might have appeared on the outside, but his apparent vigour concealed a heart struggling to keep up with the demands being placed on it by the body. Had he then gently eased off from strenuous exercise probably all might have been well; but that was not his style. If his heart needed rest then he would rest it: he swung to the other extreme, with the result that he gave himself an athlete's heart. Not only did this give him the discomfiture of palpitations, but the elimination of drink and tobacco from his life moved him, he felt, into the realm of social outcast. As he was to say:

Oh how I'd love to souse my throttle
With red wine from a dusty bottle;
Alas! my doctor says I oughter
Drink only tea and Vichy water.

Robert Service with his daughter Iris. In her opinion, he was the kindliest of men

I'd love to puff a panatella
With any other lusty fella:
Alas! if I should chance to wish one:
'Tabac's tabooed!' shrieks my physician.

Service's heart condition was to last in its physically inhibiting form for about three years. Its almost complete cure was remarkable, and he unhesitatingly gave credit for his improvement to the thermal waters of Royat where the local people are said to be the longest lived in France. He responded immediately to the treatment, his high blood pressure dropped to a normal level, and to his great delight he was told to walk eight to ten miles a day. Regularly throughout the rest of his life he would return to Royat to tone up his condition. Admittedly from now on he would be careful about his diet and the demands he placed on his body, but the challenge he gave himself, to live to be a hundred, gathered momentum from his spell at Royat. Service did not keep to himself his conviction that the waters contained health-giving properties. He enthused to such an extent that wealthy Americans flooded into Royat seeking to copy his cure. The influx of prosperity increased his local popularity. To use his daughter's words 'He was treated like a king at Royat.'

One cannot leave Service's visit to the famous watering place in the Auvergne without mentioning his unexpected encounter with someone he had not met for nearly twenty years. In the lounge of one of the hotels, Service bumped into Sir Pelham Pelham, still pursuing his Casanova activities, stoutly maintaining it was his privilege as a great-grandfather to make love to beautiful women. His ability to feast on food as well as love seems, understandably, to have promoted a feeling of inferiority in Service, and the knight's departure was a relief to him.

Service had now had a base in Paris for some fifteen years and his love affair with the city had passed beyond the passionate stage. He saw the dangers inherent in becoming, to use his own phrase, a boulevard barnacle. Dream Haven was for the summer;

Paris had been for the winter, but a few visits to the Riviera convinced him that the warmth of the Mediterranean shores was preferable to what was beginning to seem the dreary winter months of Paris. Apartments in Nice were obtained and he developed the habit of sharing the year between the Riviera and Brittany.

With his heart problem now largely behind him, Service settled down to write a book on growing old gracefully. With the title of *Why Not Grow Young*, it was to be his favourite book. He wrote it, he claimed, 'not for profit, but to do good.' And of all his non-verse books, it is the one today which is the most inviting to read. Not, it should be said, because it falls in line with so much of today's thinking about how to live healthily, but because of its easy writing style. Yet, a perverse reading public did not like it. A greying man talking about health was not what was expected of Robert William Service. A pity, but perhaps its day will come again:

> In the course of much wandering I once worked for a butcher. I must have slain thousands of poor beasts, and perhaps it is because I have taken so much life in my time I now shrink from taking any. I will step out of the way of a worm and ditch my car to avoid a yellow dog.
>
> However, it is not this insensibility that would keep me from enjoying a flesh diet. As long as I do not see it done, slaughter does not worry me. Occasionally, as when I make a meal of whitebait I have a moment of compunction to think how many beautiful little silver lives are being blurred in butter to give me a passing gustatory thrill. This doesn't bother me in the case of oysters, though I suppose the oyster enjoys his life as much as the sprat.

Writing, as he said 'not to make sick men well, but well men better', he makes the plea to draw closer to nature:

> We are all fools, only some of us know it. And knowing it we don't try

> to cure so much as to help Nature to cure. In playing roulette, never try to buck the bank. And in the increasing hazard of the years never try to buck Nature, but play more and more her game. Perhaps she doesn't care about us individually, but collectively her inflexible aim is to preserve and develop us for her own ends. She may be cruel and kill us at times, but civilisation kills us twice as fast. It is our policy to placate her. Let Nature enter more and more into our counsels.

The Riviera as a base allowed Service to explore the south of France, and once again the legs were regularly in motion as he explored the region, and especially the valleys of the Maritime Alps. He picked up an old friendship with a journalist from his pre-war Paris days and forged a new one with a former music hall star. He met other expatriate writers like H. G. Wells and Somerset Maugham.

Music had always been part of his life and now he had published his *Bath Tub Ballads*, a collection of twenty songs backed with his own musical scores. It has to be said the title of the book matched the status of the songs. But what is interesting is the indication that he still saw Scotland as his homeland:

> I'm going back to Scotland which I left when just a boy,
> For my pooch is full o' money and my heart is full of joy,
> And I'm longin' for the moment when I'll hear the porter cry,
> All change for Auchtermuchty, Eccelfechan and Mulguy.
> Chorus: All change for Auchtermuchty Eccelfechan and Mulguy.
> O that's the song I want to sing until ma throat is dry,
> And then I'll drink anither dram and I'll hae anither try.
> Sing-in' Change for Auchtermuchty, Eccelfechan and Mulguy.

Service at this time played the piano, guitar, banjo and ukelele, and now he decided it was time to learn the accordion. The motivation was there, and ultimately he reckoned he could play a hundred tunes without referring to music. He had long had pleasure from sitting in cafes listening to accordion music. Now he would grasp opportunities to spell such musicians at their work. The affection he had for his 'box' came out years later when he was to write:

Some carol of the banjo, to its measure keeping time:
Of viol or of lute some make a song.
My battered old accordion, you're worthy of a rhyme,
You've been my friend and comforter so long.
Round half the world I've trotted you, a dozen years or more;
You've given heaps of people lots of fun;
You've set a host of happy feet a-tapping on the floor-
Alas! your dancing days are nearly done.
Oh I know you're cheap and vulgar, you're an instrumental crime.
In drawing rooms you haven't got a show.
You're a musical abortion, you're the voice of grit and grime,
You're the spokesman of the lowly and the low.
You're a democratic devil, you're the darling of the mob;
You're a wheezy, breezy blasted bit of glee.
You're the headache of the high-brow, you're the horror of the snob,
But you're worth your weight in ruddy gold to me.

There is one medical event to which Service devotes a number of pages in his autobiography, and which need only be referred to here. The title he gave to the event was 'The Great Carbuncle'. The cause of the affliction was apparently his habit of twisting his shoulders in the sand as he carried out such physical exercises as shoulder stands. The result was a suppurating mess the size of a soup plate, which required much ruthless cutting out by the surgeon. His convalescence took many months.

Working his way through the newspapers one day, he came upon a reference to his own alleged death during the war. His feelings, he said, were of pleasure that his efforts at self-obliteration had succeeded; his efforts to cultivate obscurity from the general public had been successful. Presumably his name had been confused with that of his brother, and the reporter had not associated his prose writings with his verse output, whose publication Service seems to have neglected around that time. But it was an indication, nevertheless, that the public still thought of him as a rhymester. From then on, though, we see Service become more and more a very private person. His verse may be for the world to enjoy, but the less the world finds out about him, the better.

CHAPTER 9

Russian Traveller

Here let me know from human woe
The rapture of release:
The rich caress of Loveliness,
The plenitude of peace.

Atoll

IN 1930 SERVICE PAID a visit to Kilwinning, in Ayrshire. For once his lack of interest in the past seems to have been overcome. His maiden aunts had finished their lives in less than comfortable circumstances, and he reproached himself for not maintaining contact with them, and for not even providing financial support to them.

Of my good deeds I never yet
Have grudged a single one.
But Oh how deeply I regret
Good deeds I might have done.

To their memory and that of his grandfather he paid for the erection of a gravestone. He made contact with some old friends in Glasgow and then returned to Dream Haven.

It does not seem far-fetched to suggest it was with thoughts about the little shop run in Kilwinning by his grandfather and aunts that prompted the lines of *The Wee Shop* which show Service at his observant and expressive best:

I entered; how they waited all a-flutter!
How awkwardly they weighed my acid drops!
And then with all the thanks a tongue could utter

They bowed me from the kindliest of shops.
I'm sure that night their customers they numbered;
Discussed them all in happy, breathless speech;
And though quite worn and weary, ere they slumbered,
Sent heavenward a little prayer for each.

Always a master of the paddle. Robert Service with his
Canadian type canoe on the beach at Lancieux.

But that particular journey to Kilwinning over, he felt no need ever again to return to the scene of his childhood.

Even as he entered his sixties, Service retained his good figure and his ruddy complexion. Handsome in appearance and a favourite with children, increasing years did not disrupt the equanimity of his being. But his calmness could more easily pass into aloofness, and his privacy became ever more important to him. The need to write verse still dominated Service's life and if the subject matter of his verse was becoming less dramatic and more philosophical, there was to be no drop in standards. Draft followed draft until the words could be offered to the world as a professional piece of work.

Passing years did not diminish his interest in things and events one associates more with youth. Perhaps his own restlessness was a reason for it, but the French Foreign Legion fascinated him all his life. The sight of this mercenary force in their kepis and blue overcoats parading in Paris had stirred his blood, and now the urge to see them in their fighting environment came to the fore. In his verse he acknowledged the Legion as the cream of France's army, and just as his interest in the seamier side of Paris life had led him into the land of the apache, so his interest in the Legion now took him to the Regiment's headquarters at Sidi-Bel-Abbès. Of this journey he was never to report much of what he saw or did. But of his next journey, he was not slow in allowing his pen to cover the pages.

For a background to his visits to Russia, one has to remember that it is difficult, indeed impossible, to be precise about Service's politics. His claim that he never voted in his life was not made with any pride. He believed that what was earned should be kept, but his sympathies lay with the 'have-nots'. One can imagine the statement 'power corrupts' would have had his undiminished support, yet there was never any reluctance to withhold 'rendering unto Caesar', whether Caesar required his taxes, his civil obedience or even that he take care of his health.

The activities of the communists were holding his attention. He went to their meetings and read their papers. From the safety of distance he watched their confrontations. The ever-inquiring mind needed a confirmation or rejection that communism had something to offer the world. Was Russia, he wanted to know, a proletarian paradise or a mountain of misery? With some trepidation, he admitted, he made application to Intourist to visit the Soviet Union. The restless streak had again come to the fore.

Service's route to Leningrad was by way of Denmark, Sweden and Finland. The land, as he looked out from the train carrying him from Helsinki, reminded him of the Yukon. His first impressions were not greatly favourable:

All I can remember is that everything seemed very Russian. The men wore dirty blouses, top boots and peaked caps; the women shawls on their heads and shapeless skirts. There were log huts and lumber shacks, each in its neglected garden, yet with geranium plants in the windows. There were villages with low houses and wide streets. The small stations were untidy, dirty, crowded with peasants waiting for a train of any kind. The immense fields had been cropped and looked deserted in the pale sunshine. Huge farm buildings loomed on the horizon but I saw no sign of cattle.

It is typical of Service that on his arrival in Leningrad he viewed the people before the sights. And right from the beginning he displayed something akin to affection for the ordinary folk he encountered. The peasants gazing unbelievingly at the plump and dapper figures that were in his party, he noted, may have been envious of their apparent wealth but displayed no resentment. The normality of Russian women undertaking hard manual work came as something of a shock to him, and although his verse about the country is of lower quality than usual, his descriptions of what he saw are vivid:

I watched ten women from the train,
Who heavy rails were packing;
Their backs were bent to stress and strain,
Their dress was mostly sacking:
'You see,' the Comrade said to me,
'We practice Sex Equality.'

For Intourist, Service had nothing but praise. Ensconsed in the Hotel Astoria, Leningrad's finest hotel, he ignored the French bill of fare and lunched on caviar, bortsch and boiled sturgeon. While the meal satisfied him, his recollections of his room were less flattering:

By a long corridor I reached my room. A bristly valet in a dirty blouse showed me in. It was large and over-full of furniture. There was a sofa, seven chairs and a round table. Everything was dingy, faded and none too clean. The closed window gave on to a court, the air was warm and stale. The wash-basin had no plug and had become detached from the wall, so that only the water pipe held it in place. I mention this to show how everything pertaining to the old regime is being allowed to go to ruin. As a relic of Czarism the Hotel Astoria seemed to be doomed.

When one couples his comments about his room with his description of the city, one gets a fairly complete picture of Russia in the thirties.

I will never forget my first impression of Leningrad. There was an open vastness about it, a lavish spaciousness. No pedestrian proposition this. At the thought of perambulative sight-seeing my legs ached. Is there any city that offers such wide vistas and stretches with such assured majesty? True, one noted the streets needed repair, the paving was broken, the asphalt caved in. The buildings were unpainted and crumbling in decay. And the further one went the more one was conscious of poverty and neglect. Even as we thrilled at the magnificent prospect we were bumped by the roughness of the road. Even as we were roused to admiration by the monuments and mansions we were conscious of corruption and decline.

Although seeing all the mandatory sights in Leningrad, Service seems to have spent most of his time strolling round the department stores, studying the goods and the shopping habits of the people. Then it was time to prepare for his journey to Moscow. By this time he admits to having developed an affection for the shabby old Astoria and, ignoring the pleas of others in his party not to break the rules, was brazenly tipping the hotel staff.

The crush on the overnight train encouraged him to spend the journey in his berth, and he arrived in Moscow sporting a considerable stubble. The Hotel Metropole, considered at that time to be the best hotel in all Russia, was to be his base and the capital of all the Republics was to excite him much more than Leningrad. 'The Metro', with its marble staircases, sculptings of workers and soldiers and steep escalators stirred an enthusiasm within him, although he could not resist the jibe that they were 'gaudy temples to the grinning gods of proletariat progress'.

> Although I'm not devoid of malice
> And have for Bolshevics no brief,
> I must admit that like a palace,
> And beautiful beyond belief,
> The Moscow underground can claim
> The Subways of the world to shame.

Inevitably, Service joined the queue for Lenin's tomb:

> So silently and with a pretence at reverence I advanced. I was, indeed, a little nervous for the atmosphere was eerie and sinister. Solemnly we descended into semi-gloom mid dark walls of dark marble. Then, turning a corner, the air suddenly became intensely cold. It was like entering a refrigerator.
>
> We were in a long low vault. Soldiers kept moving us on. We were not allowed to hesitate a moment and our every movement was watched. We climbed half a dozen steps, halted, looked down ... we were in the presence of Lenin. We arrived at his head, walked slowly to his feet, round them, up to his head again and out. The whole business lasted less than thirty seconds and there was little time to take in any details

Nearly ten years later, Service was to recall the excursion in less serious style:

> I slouched across the great Red Square, and watched the waiting line.
> The mongrel sons of Marx were there, convened to Lenin's shrine;
> Ten thousand men of Muscovy, Mongol and Turkoman,

Black-bonnets of the Aral Sea and Tatars of Kazan.
Kalmuck and Bashkir, Lett and Finn, Georgian, Jew and Lapp,
Kirghis and Kazakh, crowding in to gaze on Lenin's map.

With all the enthusiasm of an American tourist, Service did the Moscow sights. Having now been allocated the services of an Intourist guide whose indoctrination into the wonders and benefits of communism had apparently started at the nappy stage, he found baiting her on such issues as the right to strike, non-admittance to law courts and the lack of foreign books more entertaining than cultural exhibitions and the former homes of aristocrats killed in the revolution.

But one incident induced fear in him. When walking in the street one morning an American sidled up to him. Passing Service the injunction to keep walking with his eyes straight ahead, he explained he was unable to leave the country because he had lost his papers. He pleaded with Service to memorise his brother's address in the States and request him to approach the American government for help. With a final warning that the two of them were possibly under observation he disappeared into the crowd. Coincidence or not, the next morning the party in the Metropole were advised that they were confined to the hotel. With only two days of his visa remaining, things began to look sinister. An appeal to the Intourist guide proved futile. The next day, on the grounds that a mammoth workers' celebration was scheduled, Service and his travelling companions were again confined to the hotel, although they managed to view the four-hour procession from a balcony.

The following morning the ban was removed and Service made for the Intourist office to uplift his rail ticket. There he was met with stalling from the staff, and by this time he was convinced there was a plot afoot to keep him in Russia. With an hour to spare, his ticket was handed to him. His spirits soared.

He journeyed home by Berlin. Yet within a few weeks of returning to Dream Haven, he was making plans to return to Russia. He wanted to write a novel with a Russian setting and as he tackled the first chapter the realisation came to him that he did not know enough about the country.

Again Service made his entry to Russia by train. He did not have a comfortable journey, Germany proving particularly unpleasant. At Aachen the station was mobbed by Hitler youth giving the Nazi salute and and shrieking 'Heil' with a fervid enthusiasm. War he felt, was in the air. His luggage was emptied out by the border guards and he was taken to cells under the station platform for an interrogation. With relief he boarded the Polish train although wondering why he was gallivanting in an uncouth land when he could have been basking on the beach at Dream Haven.

With his usual proneness to incidents, Service had an eventful rail journey. Before reaching Moscow he encountered amongst his fellow passengers a girl intent on assassinating Stalin with bombs she claimed were hidden in her brassiere, and his money was stolen. It was with some relief he allowed the Intourist guide to usher him to the Hotel National where he was to stay for the next few days. This time Moscow was not his goal. He was bound for Southern Russia.

Service took the train from Moscow to Gorki, where he boarded the steamer which was to take him down the Volga. 'I think it is fitting,' he wrote, 'that one's first sight of a great river should be a great moment. One should gasp and gaze. And that is what I did.' His cabin pleased him. For the next seven days until he reached Stalingrad, he relaxed, absorbed the landscape, suffered the Volga cold, and studied the boat's passengers and crew.

Stalingrad offered Service little, but Rostov, which he reached after a twenty-hour rail journey was a different prospect. Here, in what he termed the real Russia, he saw people hell-bent on enjoying themselves. The women were better dressed, food was more plentiful for the masses and music abounded. The fact that his guide was the most beautiful woman he had encountered in all Russia was merely a bonus.

Service was intent on visiting Georgia. He journeyed on to Ordzhonikidze, cursing the Soviets for giving towns such unpronounceable names, and then with a hired car, very old and battered like the provided driver, set out to cross the Caucasus Mountains. This was wild country and there is a relish in his descriptions of the journey:

Hard at work. Service at his desk, Nice 1935

In one stupendous gorge, wooded to half way up, we met a brigand-looking man in a hat of astrakan, with knives in his belt – a study in damascened daggers and dirt. He was guarding a flock of fat-tailed sheep. Another picture was a pair of donkeys, drawing a cart with their baby son running alongside. They were cute, but we had a lot of trouble to pass them. Also blocking the way were sows with young, long spouted and hairy, as they ate the roadside grass. It was amazing how the road threaded its way through these mountain barriers, muffled mistily so far above us, and all the time skirting that sheer drop to the rapids in the gorge below.

After driving through the desolation of the Georgian Pass, Service descended to something akin to another world. Here in

Georgia were girls with rosy cheeks and braids of dark hair holding out shawls for sale, throwing flowers and offering fruit. It was a laughing land with trees laden with apricots and pears. Nevertheless he was exhausted by the time he arrived in Tiflis.

For a while Service drifted somewhat aimlessly around Georgia before boarding a steamer on the Black Sea. He paid shore visits at various ports, and it was while he was in Yalta that he began to pick up worrying news about the political situation in Europe. He continued his tour and a day later came the news that Germany and Russia had signed a non-aggression pact. This brought home to him the seriousness of the plight that now faced Poland. He realised he could have problems in getting home. The boat journey to Odessa and then on to Kiev seemed interminable. At Kiev, after strenuous efforts, he managed to book a rail ticket to Warsaw with the intention of continuing his journey to Brittany by way of Berlin and Paris. Thinking he would now be home within a few days, he celebrated by having a second breakfast.

It was while changing trains at the Russian-Polish frontier that Service got the news that Poland and the Reich were now at war. One feels that in the extremely unpleasant position Service now found himself in, the natural decision would have been to make direct for somewhere like Lithuania to seek a boat passage to a Scandinavian country. But that was not his choice. He elected to go on to Warsaw where he would see German planes flying unopposed over the city:

> I was in Warsaw when the first bomb fell;
> I was in Warsaw when the terror came –
> Havoc and horror, famine, fear and flame,
> Blasting from loveliness a living hell.
> Barring the station towered a sentinel;
> Trainward I battled, blind escape my aim.
> England! I cried. He kindled at the name:
> With lion-leap he haled me... All was well.

On the advice of the British Consul he made for Estonia which he reached after a protracted rail journey, and there took ship for Stockholm. A civilised rail journey to Bergen restored his equilibrium. There he booked a sea passage to England.

If Service thought his troubles were now all over he was mistaken. To get home to France he now needed a visa, and in those early war years such things were not handed out for the asking. But at least the post allowed contact with his family.

The Imperial Hotel
Russell Square
London
Sunday

Dear Family,

You see I am writing every day because there is not much else to do. I am hanging around waiting for a permit to go home and feeling quite cheerful about it as I am at this moment gorged with a huge hotel breakfast. I am living like a prince with a pocketful of money. So it all feels like heaven after all I went through to get here. I have a lovely room and am being well looked after. Tomorrow I will have some shirts washed and a suit pressed. They need it.

London looks very funny. Nine out of ten people carry gas masks on the street. I went to get one but they had not my size so I am going again tomorrow. The shops have sandbags piled up in front and their windows crossed with adhesive tape. But there are very few uniforms to be seen and everyone seems cheerful. The hotel is quite empty.

If you go away before I get over, get Poulard to fix up my motor as usual. I still think it would be better to take the train to Nice. It does not seem right to use petrol at this moment even if one can get it. Above all, guard my manuscript of verse. It is to be published in February. I am starting a novel right away to be published in August.

I saw my publisher and they are keen about it. Well, I'll finish my Sunday papers and I'll go for a walk to Shaftsbury Avenue. Expect my daily bulletin to-morrow.

Besto - Bobovitch

Service arrived in Paris to discover his family were in Nice, and because it was in a war zone he could not go there. He fumed and tried and made use of contacts, but to no avail. The story should finish with his own words:

Then I thought I would at least have a try, so with my bag I went to the Gare de Lyon and calmly demanded a ticket for Nice. Sure! They handed me one at once, and in another moment I was on the train. It was as easy as all that. And after a night passed comfortably in a Wagon-lit compartment, the prodigal father arrived in the forenoon and surprised his family sitting down to lunch.

CHAPTER I

Refugee to Hollywood

Let laureates sing with a rapturous swing
Of the wonder and glory of work;
Let pulpiteers preach and with passion impeach
The indolent wretches who shirk.
No doubt they are right: in the stress of the fight
It's the slackers who go to the wall;
So though it's my shame I perversely proclaim
It's fine to do nothing at all.

Laziness

SERVICE AND HIS FAMILY spent the winter of 1939-40 on the Riviera. In his own words, 'I spent that winter strolling around Nice in my Saville Row suits and giving birth to another book of verse.' The family moved from their apartment into a large and gracious house in the Place Franklin previously owned by Gaston Leroux, author of *The Mystery of the Yellow Room*, a connoisseur piece for detective novel enthusiasts.

Peter McQuattie, Service's journalist friend from his Paris days, who had also taken up residence on the Riviera, died that winter, and was buried near D.H. Lawrence, whom Service appeared to have known slightly. Life, though, was dominated by the war, even if it was being referred to, due to almost total inaction, as 'the phony war.'

Behind the Maginot Line with its concrete gun emplacements and underground ammunition stores, all connected by a labyrinth of tunnels supposedly impenetrable to gunfire, France felt secure. But Mussolini's territorial demands for part of the Riviera concerned Service, and the decision was taken to return to Brittany. It was while the family were on their way north that the Blitzkrieg struck. Long before they reached the peace of Dream Haven they were to hear first hand stories from refugees of the horrors of the Stuka dive bombings in Belgium, and see the pathetic sight of refugees on the road with their belongings.

Then came a stream of ever-worsening news; the Germans had crossed the Meuse: nothing seemed capable of stopping the Panzers. The King of Belgium ordered capitulation. France made an appeal to America for help. Mounting his motor-bike, Service made for St Malo to obtain more news of the situation. There, the sight of British troops being evacuated to England convinced him the war on the continent would shortly be over.

Returning home he told his wife and daughter that they were going to get out; their luggage would have to be limited to a suit-case each. The main routes now being blocked with refugee traffic, Service used his local knowledge to reach St Malo by various side roads. He parked his blue Lancia in the town and sought out the naval officer in charge of embarkation. They were allocated to the HULL TRADER making for Weymouth. Aghast, they watched wounded troops being stacked on top of the ship's load of high explosives, and the ships around them being loaded right down to the gunwales with remnants of the British Expeditionary Force being taken home to continue the fight.

Shortly after arriving in England, Service took over the lease of an apartment in Chelsea. But London was not a natural habitat for Service. There was little reason for him to remain in Britain, and a few weeks later the family experienced the eeriness of sailing down the Mersey in war-time. On board were a thousand children being evacuated to Canada or America for their safety. The fates seem to have been guarding Service at this time, as both the London flat and the ship which carried him across the Atlantic were shortly afterwards to succumb to enemy action.

Service landed in Montreal, where he was unexpectedly met by his brother Stanley whom he had not seen for many years. Equally unexpectedly his sister Agnes appeared on his doorstep in Vancouver. But Canada was not to be his domicile. Ever the sunlover, his eyes were set on California, and the family settled in a modest house in Hollywood which was to be their home for the next five years. Unable to get access to most of his funds because of war-time restrictions, the simple life he claimed always to prefer was forced upon him. His *Bar Room Ballads*, which he had started in Nice, was published in 1940, and he soon found himself involved in the promotional exercises associated with the launch of a new book.

Of all Service's books of verse, none have provided such a hotchpotch mixture as *Bar Room Ballads*. The verse, without apparent logic, ranges from the ridiculous to the serious, from the Yukon to France, from a smattering of the Scots tongue to refined English. But it does contain some gems, including Grandad, one of the most delightful pieces he was ever to write:

Heaven's mighty sweet, I guess;
Ain't no rush to git there;
Been a sinner more or less;
Maybe wouldn't fit there.
Wicked still, bound to confess;
Might jest pine a bit there.

– Here I weed the garden plot,
Scare the crows from pillage;
Simmer in the sun a lot,
Talk about the tillage.
Yarn of battles I have fought,
Greybeard of the village.

Lord, I know You'll understand.
With Your Light You'll lead me.
Though I'm not the pious brand,
I'm here when you need me,
Gosh! I know that Heavens grand,
But dang it! God, don't speed me.

The year 1940 also saw the death in Alberta of Sam McGee. For years he had to put up with enquiries as to whether the weather was hot enough for his satisfaction.

To begin with at least, Service led a life of reasonable seclusion in Hollywood. He read, played his accordion and walked for a couple of hours every day; a habit considered idiosyncratic by the population of a town apparently born with wheels instead of feet.

As he grew older, Robert Service never lost his ability to look comfortable in whatever he was wearing

After lounging around for a year, Service started to become more involved in the community. He gave recitations of his works, delivered talks to clubs and societies and accepted invitations to broadcast. Radio had an attraction for him, and he developed a good microphone voice, although he admits when he heard his own voice played back for the first time he thought he sounded like Harry Lauder. His slight Scottish burr, of course, stayed with him for all of his life.

Having experienced and indeed enjoyed the flow of money from the film rights for several of his literary efforts, Service was in no mood to refuse a telephone invitation to meet again with Frank Lloyd, the film director he had worked with twenty years previously. Lloyd at the time was working on a remake of *The Spoilers,* a film about the north, which would star John Wayne, Marlene Dietrich and Randolph Scott. The director thought it would be interesting and would add a bit of colour (if not authenticity) to the film, if, in a dance hall scene, Service could appear writing one of his Yukon ballads.

With the confidence that springs from ignorance of what is involved, he accepted. Being made up as a younger man, he recalls, wasn't too bad, as the make-up artist had been responsible for transforming Boris Karloff into Frankenstein. His main difficulty was in finding a costume that didn't make him appear as a Keystone comedy actor. Then having learned the few phrases required of him, he had to absorb the instructions given: *'Don't try to act – Don't try to be a bloody Barrymore.'* Sixteen times, he recalled, the sultry seduction voice of Dietrich put him off his stride. The seventeenth brought success, 'It's lousy but we'll let it go,' was the comment ringing in his ears as he left the set.

Service was not invited to benefit Hollywood with his acting talents again. But reading his autobiography one is left in no doubt that the most pleasure he obtained from his visit to the studio was not his own performance, but watching the great film fight that takes place in *The Spoilers* between John Wayne and Randolph Scott. As usual, there was an expression in verse:

Johnny Wayne and Randy Scott
They fought and fought and fought and fought.
With joy they shed each other's gore,
And then they paused and shed some more...

The film set, with the miners in huckskin, the dance hall girls and the general mixture of types which frequent a mining camp seems to have evoked some nostalgia for the Yukon. But he was not to use his presence on the North American continent as an excuse to revisit his old haunts in the north. He had left the Yukon promising to return, to be true to the land which had given him so much, so why did he not return to the scenes of his early inspirations; to walk again from Whitehorse to Myles Canyon, to stare at the beauties of Emerald Lake; to reminisce by Five Fingers Rapids? Nothing at that time or later indicated that he had forgotten the Yukon. But his claim that he did not want to see Dawson as a ghost town can only provide a partial reason for not returning. The town was beginning its decline before he left the Yukon.

To find the true reason we have rather to look at Service the man. Diffident and indolent are just two of the adjectives which may be applied to him, but they reflect the philosophy which stayed with him all his life. And another constant trait was that he did not look back. Water which had flowed under the bridge was water which had flowed away; the here and now, the present, was ever more important than the past. And while the past could be enjoyed in the shape of nostalgia, it was best left in that state of limbo where the good memories transcended the bad. Remember his lines from *Goodbye, Little Cabin*.

> – How cold, still and lonely, how weary you seem.
> A last wistful look and I'll go.
> Oh will you remember the lad with its dream!
> The lad that you comforted so.
> The shadows enfold you, It's drawing to-night
> The evening star needles the sky.
> And huh! but it's stinging and stabbing my sight –
> God Bless you, old cabin, goodbye!

The Yukon also offered no human links of importance. Not that these were ever all that vital to him. While his few friendships were strong, he saw little need to continue acquaintanceships, and even the family ties with his brothers and sisters were allowed to become tenuous. We have to conclude that his reasons for not returning to the Yukon whilst living in America have more to do with the mould of the man than the physical deterioration of Dawson.

His wife, though, was of a different character, and was not one to pass up an opportunity. During a visit to Vancouver in the summer of 1942, Mrs Service accepted an invitation extended by the steamship side of the Canadian Pacific Railway company to visit her husband's old cabin in Dawson. With daughter Iris she travelled up the Inside Passage and completed the journey to Dawson, first by the narrow-gauge Whitehorse Railway and then by paddle steamer, a journey she was still to describe years later as 'one I had never dared hope for and one I shall never forget.' Service's cabin at the time was being cared for by The Daughters Of The Empire, and Mrs Service confessed to feeling emotional when she saw, 'the moose horns over the porch out-stretched like arms.' Sheets of paper which Service used for the writing of his poems were still hanging on the wall, but her practical nature was soon to take over. '*Ça m'a fait triste,*' she said, and was not impressed by the uneven wooden floor. It is not known whether the can of Berna condensed milk which provided the name of the heroine in his Trail of '98 was on show.

The somewhat gentle existence Service was living in Hollywood was brought to an end in an unusual way. His wife was attending English classes at the local High School, and waiting in the school corridor to meet her one evening, he became aware that a teacher was leading a discussion on poetry. More than that, the teacher was proclaiming Service to have no standing as a poet, whilst one of the students, an elderly man, was putting up a spirited defence for the reading of Service on the grounds that he whetted the appetite for tackling major poets. More than a little interested, he quietly slipped into the back of the class to listen to the discussion.

Ignoring the wisdom of discretion he entered the argument, finishing up by disclosing his identity. With a liking for the people he was now involved with, he entered the world of amateur poets, speaking at their meetings and conventions until he found himself leading the busy life which so antagonised his soul. A break had to be made; a reason for leaving the company of a number of people he had come to like had to be found. The means of evasion he chose to enable him to return to the hermit's existence was the writing of an autobiography, and this he announced to all and sundry; from now on until the job was done he would be incommunicado.

There is romance attached to writing in a garret, and at least dignity is present when the author operates from the comfort of a well-carpeted, book-lined study. Somewhat incongruously, Service's choice was to work in his garage, with his typewriter perched on the end of a trunk.

Writing of course involves thinking, and thinking with Service required the prompting of exercise. At least, due to the length of American cars, he was not short of room in which to pace, and a regular morning's output of two thousand words indicated that both the physical and intellectual man were functioning at peak performance.

Service's fellow Scots-Canadian, Lord Beaverbrook, used to contend that no one should attempt an autobiography before the age of seventy, on the grounds that up to that time one's career and philosophy could change dramatically. Service had no such fears. He was not plagued with thoughts of success sourly fuming to failure, nor did he think an autobiography should concern itself with giving advice to the young. Punching away on his typewriter, Service set out to record the sequence of his life, warts and all. He wrote in such detail that he was soon to discover he had enough material for two books. He resolved to limit his story to the first forty years of his life, and the autobiography, which took a year to write, was given the title of *Ploughman Of The Moon*. Then came an extended period of revision and checking and arguing over galley proofs which, according to his daughter, showed the perfectionist streak in him. But his trials were not yet over – his publishers demanded their pound of flesh in publicity terms, and public appearances were the order of the day.

Hateful of publicity though he may have been, when necessary he could rise to the occasion better than he ever suggested in his books, and store signing sessions, bun feasts, baby shows and lecture hall engagements were attended with a smiling face. 'Peering into bookshops,' he said, 'I would watch the pile of my books grow lower, wondering why people bought them, and worrying lest that poor trusting guy, the bookseller, would get stuck. If he had, I think I would have bought them myself.'

Service had started to write *Ploughman Of The Moon* when the war news was not far removed from the doom and gloom period. But the summer after the launch of his book saw the end of the war in Europe and for the next few months Service and his wife were to live with the exile's pain of longing for home. A pain, it has to be said which was not shared by their daughter. Iris was now in her twenties, and had spent most of her teenage years in the States. According to her father, she was a 'poet of the pantry, an artist of the ironing table.' The crude inefficiency of the Old World had not the same beckoning appeal for her that it had for her parents, but she was too much of a dutiful daughter to allow them to return home without her, knowing full well the problems that would await them in France.

So, after visas to return to France were received, the family packed up, said *adieu* to their Hollywood home and set out to cross America by train to New York. After a short spell there, they found passage on a ship bound for Marseilles.

CHAPTER 11

The End of the Trail

These will I sing, and if one of you linger
Over my pages in the Long, Long Night,
And on some lone line lay a callous finger,
Saying 'It's human-true – it hits me right';
Then will I count this loving toil well spent;
Then will I dream awhile – content, content.

To The Man Of The High North

WHILE WITHOUT THE U-BOAT danger of the Atlantic crossing in the reverse direction some five years earlier, the journey back to France appears to have been unmitigated misery. There was a howling gale and the ship was empty. It bobbed like the proverbial cork. Three days before the Services embarked, the ship had disgorged its load of fifteen hundred G.I.s, and on its return journey to pick up another load, found its great bulk occupied by only fifteen civilians, who were aghast at the labyrinth of wire mattresses and metallic bracings in which they were expected to exist. The exercise area-cum-salon was a tarpaulin-covered hold, and Service, having borrowed an accordion from a friendly steward, passed the days there. A film was shown every evening, and by coincidence Service saw himself on the screen in *The Spoilers* in mid-ocean.

Towards the end of the crossing, Service picked up a flu-like condition, and as the ship threaded its way through the sunken ships in Marseilles harbour became more discomforted. The pitiful condition of the inhabitants, the absence of hotel rooms, the cold weather, all contributed to a feeling of misery, but as the

THE END OF THE TRAIL

coast train ran past the familiar stations his spirits rose. At last they reached Nice. The assistance of a porter with a barrow was obtained. Full of nervousness they made for their house. They had no way of knowing in what condition they would find it. In the place Franklin every house save one had been looted: the exception was Service's. The same concierge they had known for years admitted them; they were home.

That first winter in Nice had little to commend it. Shortage of food was their main concern, and modest as the Services could be in their eating habits, the change from the quantity and range of American meats and vegetables to what was available in their war-torn area was painful. Despondent they stood in the line queuing for the little that was available, praying all the while that the food would not run out before they reached the counter. That first Christmas dinner at home, Service's daughter recalls, consisted of one sardine and some potatoes.

But slowly things got better for the family, if not so quickly for their neighbours. Because of his citizenship Service was eligible for Red Cross parcels, and friends in the States sent them food parcels. And as the Riviera sun began to warm the land, the people as well as the crops responded. At the May Festival of the Flowers the population showed that while they could not forget the atrocities of the occupation they could at least be thankful for what they had. And as the American occupation troops slowly took their leave and the odd visitor appeared on the Promenade des Anglais, Nice, a step at a time, resumed to its old glory. Service, responding to the change for the better, turned his thoughts to the north. He had been happy with what he had found intact in his Riviera home. How had Dream Haven fared?

One of the ironies of life is how the truly unimportant frequently occupies our attention to a disproportionate degree. With Service it was his car. He had been a keen motorist in an era when motoring was a sporting pastime with a status difficult to comprehend, far less accept, today. Many of his happiest hours had been spent behind the wheel touring Europe with his family.

Service developed a real love for the blue Lancia he had obtained a few years before the war started. This was the car that had carried the family to St Malo to be left on the quayside as they hurried to embark for England. From the local garage owner who shared Service's affection for the car came the news that his car had survived the war. And somewhat ridiculously, it was this news that seemed to provide the final bit of encouragement needed to return to Brittany.

With pride, the garage owner described how he had defended the car from the Germans. He had removed and hidden tyres, partially dismantled it when it was likely to be appropriated, and claimed it as his own – a dangerous claim to make, since being found out in such action carried the possibility of transportation or worse.

The Services found at Dream Haven that the Germans had been particularly severe on the population. Being on the coast, security demanded a compliant population. The Commandant of the village had been a singularly nasty character. Old British people who had elected to remain in France were shipped off to concentration camps. Imprisonment for slight offences was common. The total destruction of the village was threatened for misdemeanour. It is obvious that in leaving before the occupation, Service took the right decision for the protection of his family and himself. His own words suggest what might have been his lot had he stayed:

> ... No sooner had we gone than the Germans surged on the scene. The road was stiff with their cars. 'Where is the Englishman,' they cried, 'who writes bad things about our Fuhrer?'...

> Soon the Commandant appeared. A slim man about my height, he, too, sported a monocle. 'This place pleases me,' he said. 'I will make it my headquarters.' Then he looked at my shelves of books, remarking 'If I were not a German soldier it would please me to be an English gentleman. But this author is an enemy of my country. In his books does he not call us Huns! Well, if ever we are obliged to quit this charming spot we will leave behind us only a shambles.'

Robert Service and Germaine at the door of 'Dream Haven'.
Even in old age, his athleticism was obvious.

> So saying he selected the best of my Saville Row suits, my pearl grey and chalk lined blue flannels and strutted through the village. Then began the joyous loot in which all of value we possessed vanished overnight. Our silver and napery, our linen, embroidery, pictures, our carpets, curtains, clothes and shoes
>
> With what sadistic joy they discovered my accordion under the roof beam where I had hidden it. My grand piano, a Steinway, was shipped to Hamburg; my guitars, my motor cycle were grabbed with delight.

Dream Haven was to suffer more than looting. It was converted into a strong point, and the walls were breached to allow wide arcs for machine gun fire. The fact that it was not totally destroyed by American troops as they drove the Germans from the village can only be attributed to good fortune.

For thirty years Dream Haven had been Service's anchor, and its virtual destruction and the loss of his books, musical instruments and personal belongings hurt him badly. Now in his seventies he must have found it difficult, especially in the austerity conditions of post-war Europe, to have complete faith in his vow that he would return Dream Haven to its former self. But the attempt was made, and every summer saw him there, seeking to recapture the gifts of loafing and writing, reading and making music which nature had decreed as his forms of happiness.

The loner in Service came evermore to the fore as the years passed. His existence became more like that of a hermit. A prolific letter writer, while willing to enter into correspondence with many and any, he sternly restricted meetings with people, from academics to enthusiasts for his works, who wished to visit him. Only occasionally did he show interest in his relations outwith his immediate family circle. Writing to one Ayrshire relative he recalled his second cousin who had achieved a modicum of fame as a twice-serving Premier of the Colony of Victoria, as it was then, in Australia. Surprisingly he never sought to record stories of his interesting relatives, like that cousin who had presided over the First Federal Conference of Australia, or the one known in the family as 'The Eminent Divine'.

The villagers in Lancieux remember Service at this time as a well-dressed, slightly formal and dapper figure, walking regularly, and greeting everyone with politeness but reserve. Although he was never overtly involved in village affairs, the mayor remembers him as always being interested in knowing if there was anything he could do to improve village life. He was recognised as a bene-factor; the war memorial and the furnishing of the village school were his major contributions. A suitable response from the authorities was the naming of a street after him.

The second half of his autobiography was now his main pre-occupation, and this he completed while enjoying the delights of Dream Haven. Although more than reasonably active for his age, the end of the book indicates his acceptance of his years. 'When I was young,' he wrote, 'I had three ambitions, to make a million dollars, to write twenty books, to live to be a hundred. The last I will never do. I will have to content myself with a modest ninety.' And his mental alertness suggested that might be a possibility. Writing to the Annual Banquet of the Vancouver Yukoners' Association in 1957 he said:

Far in my sunny southern home
I stare across the fairy foam
In pensive mood;
In spirit at the very least,
I'm with you at your merry feast
Of Brotherhood.
And here, in seven years from now,
I'll still be one of you, I vow,
A wise old guy;
I'll prove that Yukon hearts are stout;
With you at ninety and not out,
Age I'll defy.

Invited to attend the following year, no lessening of spirit was noticeable:

Please assure the vintage Sourdoughs I am with them in heart and spirit (or spirits) though I am obliged to cultivate slow motion in my movements. I wish I could hail the old gang with cheer, but the best we can do is to wish them well for another year. So bless us all once again with guts and grit. MUSH ON!

With kindest regards.

When I was a Klondike high roller
I tilted my poke with the best
And though the climate might be polar
I'd plenty of hair on my chest.
Now while I've no trace of rheumatics,
And maybe I shouldn't complain,
I'm worried because I ain't what I was,
And I wish I was eighty again.
Some claim that the nineties are naughty,
Them statements I grieve to reverse;
You've got to be humble not haughty
To jiggety-jog of the hearse.
I blink at the blonde in bikini,
I shrink from the wink of champagne...
But reforming, by heck! What a pain in the neck!
Gosh!
I wish I was eighty again!

The following month he was to write to a friend on Vancouver Island:

I am now in my eighty-fifth year and have no excessive infirmities, and am very proud because I have passed the winter without a single cold. My legs and lungs are the first to make me feel age-conscious but I have no doubt they will carry me over the ninety mark.

I work harder than ever and the day I quit will be my dying one.

A few weeks later he was filmed by CBC for a television programme. The interviewer was Pierre Berton, and Service remembered his mother well from their Yukon days. Berton was to experience Service's desire for perfection. Service presented him with a script on arrival and told him to go and learn his lines, adding the rider that Berton had the smaller part because it was his, Service's show. During the filming, Service was full of high spirits and eager to make the event last as long as possible. Perhaps he realised it would be his last appearance on film.

Service was not to achieve his ambition to reach the ninety mark.

Robert Service died in his beloved Dream Haven in the September of 1958. His death was recorded in newspapers throughout the world. There was recognition that Service had filled a unique place in literature. The following year a monument was erected to his memory near to the tennis club where he had spent so much time at Cowichan on Vancouver Island. And as already reported, the people of Lancieux were in later years to erect a plaque to his memory in the main street of the town.

Service's family continued his life style of wintering on the Riviera and spending summer in Brittany. Mrs Service was to achieve a great age. In 1981 she wrote to the editor of *The Star* in the Yukon saying she had had to give up reading the paper because her eyesight was failing, and that she had moved into a home. To the end she was to retain all her faculties. She died in Monte Carlo on the 26th December 1989 at the age of a hundred and two.

Although Dream Haven is now boarded up, Service's daughter is still a regular visitor to Lancieux. A sun-worshipper like her father, she spends most of her time on the Riviera.

In the closing pages of *Harper of Heaven* Service not unexpectedly philosophises in some depth. Such is the prerogative of a person of advanced years. Then, imperceptibly, a change is noticed. The words, the emotions are his, but it is as if there is an additional inspiration at work. His final page of prose makes beautiful reading. It is a fitting cairn to mark the End of the Trail:

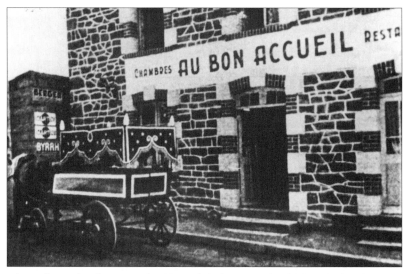

According to local custom, the driver of the hearse had a drink in *Au Bon Accueil*, before taking the coffin from the church to the cemetery.

Happiness in whatever form it comes is not to be questioned. It is to be hugged to the heart. Illusion is to be cherished. On the surface is enchantment enough ...

Surely a faith in our Universe and our human destiny should satisfy us. Let us then put all futile gropings for a meaning of life out of our minds and come down to the pure joy of living. Let us worship Nature as she reveals herself in all simplicity and beauty. And if we live in usefulness and sanity according to her laws, cultivating happiness and sharing it with those near and dear to us, we will do more than well. The measure of our sunshine is the brightness we can kindle in the eyes of others.

In some cloistered garden we may walk with peace, and in the joy of little things our vain efforts to comprehend the Universe may be forgotten. In tangible beauty is charm and solace. In visible nature is comfort. Let us be eager to be pleased; grateful for every gleam of sunshine. Nature can comfort us and bring us joy. Are we not her children? Let us try, if it so pleases us, to understand her with the mind of sages, but let us enjoy her with the hearts of children.

So in the end let us seek a quiet home, and with earth radiant about us, face the setting sun. With thankful eyes and grateful hearts let us rejoice it has been granted to us to live the length of our years in a world of beauty – to understand much, to divine much, and to come at last through pleasant paths to peace. Peace and understanding! So with our last gaze let us face the serene sunset, content to have played our parts and saying humbly:

Nature from whose bosom I come, take me back tenderly, lovingly, forgive my faults, my failures, and now that my usefulness to you is ended, grant me to rest eternally.

ALL IS WELL

CHAPTER 12

Don't Call Me a Poet

For God's sake don't call me a poet
for I've never been guilty of that

IT WAS ALWAYS SERVICE'S CLAIM that he wrote verse for those who wouldn't be seen dead reading poetry. It was a wise enough statement for the world's largest seller of verse to make. He had, after all, a proven recipe for financial success. But his pen was too prolific, his rhyming too much of a hobby, for the production of poetry which would stand comparison with the masters. Many poets have written so much that the amount of mediocre work has swamped their claim to genius. James Hogg, the Ettrick Shepherd, is one that comes readily to mind. Service did not merely write a great deal, he just never stopped producing. And rhyming came to him almost as easily as talking does to the rest of us. Inevitably, one is reminded of Robert Burns, in his Epistle to John Lapraik:

I am nae poet, in a sense;
But just a rhymer like by chance,
An' hae to learning nae pretence;
Yet, what the matter?
Whene'er my muse does on me glance,
I jingle at her.

Anyone attempting to assess the place in literature of Robert Service has ruthlessly to cut and discard huge amounts of his work before putting forward a claim for status in terms of 'literary recognition'.

Many of course already consider Service to be worthy of a poet's crown. His *Rhymes of a Red Cross Man* is widely accepted in America to be the finest collection of war poems to come from the First World War. This collection headed the non-fiction best-seller lists in 1917 and 1918. Witter Bhymer, when reviewing the book wrote:

> Robert W. Service has been a poetic phenomenon. More or less ignored by the critics, he has won a vast following. And it would seem to me time for a fellow craftsman to protest that in this case the public is right. We have been inquiring for the poetry of the war. In my judgment, here it is.

To read the first few lines of *A Casualty* is to realise that Bhymer was not mistaken:

> That boy I took in the car last night,
> With the body that awfully sagged away,
> And the lips blood-crisped, and the eyes flame-bright,
> And the poor hands folded and cold as clay –
> Oh, I've thought and I've thought of him all the day.

In the august halls of academia Service had the accolade of 'Poet' placed on his shoulders when some Yale students voted him second after Tennyson as their favourite poet. The knowledge that his works have been translated into languages as diverse as Norwegian and Italian prompts the thought that some nationalities are perhaps not so pedantic as the English speaking countries when it comes to defining poets and poetry.

Thomas Carlyle, the Sage of Chelsea, considered poetry to be 'musical thought'. Voltaire was attracted to poetry because it was capable of saying, 'more and in fewer words than prose'. Matthew Arnold's statement that, 'poetry is simply the most beautiful, impressive and widely effective mode of saying things' has been widely accepted. G.K. Chesterton, the arch-commentator, has come up with a statement about poetry which appears to strengthen Service's standing:

> Poetry is not a selection of the images which will express a particular thought; rather it is an analysis of the thoughts which are evoked by a certain image. The metaphor, the symbol, the picture, has appeared to most critics to be a mere ornament, a piece of moulding above the gateway; but it is actually the keystone of the arch. Take away the particular image employed and the whole fabric of thought falls with a crash.

In one major dictionary, poetry is defined as a composition in verse, usually characterised by concentrated and heightened language in which words are chosen for their sound and suggestive power as well as for their sense, and using such techniques as metre, rhyme and alliteration. That Service was a master of metre and rhyme is surely not in question. And who would deny that Service has an ability to choose his words with an incisiveness that raises his readers' powers of visualisation to their peak?

> So poor the room, so small, so scant,
> Yet somehow oh, so bright and airy.
> There was a pink geranium plant,
> Likewise a very pert canary.
> And in the maiden's heart it seemed
> Some fount of gladness must be springing,
> For as alone I sadly dreamed
> I heard her singing, singing, singing.

The issue as to whether or not to call Service a poet must largely depend on what is construed to be heightened language. And that depends on the reader's own base line. It may be a reflection on Service's own cultural position, which, be it remembered, was significant, that he never considered himself a poet. But let us recognise that the ordinary man in the street would have disagreed with him. To Service, Keats was the master poet:

> Your little book of limp green leather

I sadly fear that I profane,
Because we two are linked together
In this rococo hall of gain
And golden Asti I'll be spilling
To your sweet memory, god willing,
Divine John Keats;
Aye, fluted glasses I'll be filling
To toast you, Keats.

This was poor stuff for Service to offer his hero, but it is instructive in that it indicates to what extent Service was his own man. The poet Keats grew ever onward and upward. Service continued over the years to trundle out rhymes and verse that displayed a healthy average. Similar spirits in terms of manliness, sensitivity and modesty they may have been, but writing and rhyming was too much part of Service for the urge to produce something that would unequivocally be recognised and accepted as poetry to surface. Indeed at times one almost feels that when his verse is becoming so good that it must be poetry, he pulls back to what he knows the man in the street will like. One wonders what might have been achieved if wealth had not come to him so relatively easily and so early in life. If garret life had been forced on him, would the struggle to survive have produced verse of greater quality? Or would his preference for half the work and half the salary have dominated all else?

It is of course common practice to liken Service to Kipling more than to any other poet. Many articles refer to Service as the Kipling of the North, and suggest he moulded himself on the author of *Barrack Room Ballads*. Yet in *Ploughman of the Moon*, Service states quite clearly he aped Keats for sonnets, and Austin Dobson for ballads, and that Tennyson and Browning provided his poetic taste. Those latter two indicate a divergence of taste, for, as Chesterton points out in his *Handful of Authors*, Browning had literally a passion about ideas, while Tennyson had, not a passion about ideas, but ideas about passion. Service admits to reading Kipling whilst in the Yukon: but to what extent did Kipling have a direct influence on him? Kipling was born in 1865, only nine years before Service. His *Barrack Room Ballads*, the work most likely to have had an influence on Service, was published in 1892. In a jingoistic age, that book achieved tremendous popularity, and as Kipling had already attained literary recognition with such creditable tales as *Soldiers Three and The Light That Failed*, the public was ready to accept a lack of refinement in the poetic form which was more than compensated for by vigour of diction and swing of rhythm. Why is it that Service only seemed to come to terms with Kipling later in life?

> I'm dreaming tonight in the fireglow,
> Alone in my study tower,
> My books battalioned around me, my
> Kipling flat on my knee.

Was it because in his early years Service was not cast in the jingoistic mould? There are grounds for thinking that this is so. Certainly in his early years in British Columbia he did not consider that just being British was a superior qualification. At the time *Barrack Room Ballads* was published, Service was himself going through his socialist phase. It is at least a possibility that this inhibited his liking for Kipling at the time. And it is worth noting that the Kipling poem Service admitted to reciting most in later years was *Gunga Din*, the story of the water carrier who, at the end of the day, proved he was the equal of any Sahib.

Or did Service feel his verse already to be the equal of Kipling's? Service's diffidence at times conceals a streak of confidence, even conceit, about his ability to hold his own in many situations. With the assurance of youth he may have considered the newspaper-man working in India, as Kipling was at the time, to be producing nothing better than he was himself. He had achieved publication: perhaps it was only a matter of time before he achieved fame comparable to Kipling's. Or are we just to say that Kipling's fame left Service cold; he had other fish to fry. Service's daughter, on reflection, thinks too much has been made of Kipling's influence on her father. Other poets figured more prominently in his conversation.

But for all the definitions as to what does and what does not constitute poetry, the reading public seems to have an expectation as to what poetry should be about. Glorious deeds or pictures of flowers bending in the wind, philosophies and mother love, satirical expression and fantasising – these are the anticipated contents between the covers of a book defined as poetry. To all these Service could give attention. But he had to go further and, like Burns, bring the common and everyday into his work. Service was primarily an observer, and incident and ambience were his building blocks. Sam McGee is perhaps the classic example:

> The Northern Lights have seen queer sights,
> But the queerest they ever did see
> Was that night on the marge of Lake Lebarge
> I cremated Sam McGee

In *Julot the Apache*, he wastes no time in introducing both the characters and the story:

> And that was how I came to know Julot and Gigolette,
> And we would talk and drink a bock, and smoke a cigarette.
> And I would meditate upon the artistry of crime,
> And he would tell of cracking cribs and cops and doing time.

Service here cannot be accused of using either heightened language or the expected raw material of poetry; it is the rhythm that carries us along and stimulates the desire for more.

Even when he turns to material more in line with what the ordinary person expects from poetry, he so often diverts on to a side track:

> I have some friends, some worthy friends,

And worthy friends are rare:
These carpet slippers on my feet,
That padded leather chair.

Service of course loved to make use of the twist in the tale and the unexpected punch line. In *My Madonna*, he magnificently exploits this ability. The story starts with a prostitute posing for an artist:

I hailed me a woman from the street,
Shameless, but, oh, so fair!
I bade her sit in the artist's seat,
And I painted her sitting there.

An art critic visits the studio, and, commenting on the woman's beauty, the artist is prompted to review the setting of the painting:

So I painted a halo round her hair,
And I sold her and took my fee,
And she hangs in the Church of Saint Hilaire,
Where you and all may see.

Service's interest in amateur dramatics has been touched on earlier. In *Cafe Comedy* he introduces a touch of theatre to the dialogue. In this, one of his most delightful pieces, a man and a woman have arranged to meet in a cafe with a view to matrimony. They will recognise each other by the wearing of a flower. A sense of trepidation has caused both to give the other the impression that they are much younger than they really are. Thus they wait in the cafe with a growing sense of despondency, until:

– suddenly they turned, to start and stare.
She spied a marguerite, he glimpsed a rose;
Their eyes were joined and in a flash they knew –

If Service had maintained this standard throughout his long career then his standing as a poet would have been assured. Again, his work possesses a charisma that one associates with Burns. It is interesting to compare the way Burns and Service handle a similar theme. From Burns's *Epistle to a Young Friend*:

I'll no say, men are villains a':
The real, harden'd wicked,
Wha hae nae check but human law,
Are to the few restricted:
But Och, mankind are unco weak,
An' little to be trusted;
If self the wavering balance shake,
It's rarely right adjusted!

In *The Men That Don't Fit In*, Service wrote:

If they went straight they might go far;
They are strong and brave and true;
But they're always tired of the things that are,
And they want the strange and new
They say, 'Could I find my proper groove,
What a deep mark I would make!'
So they chop and change, and each fresh move
Is only a fresh mistake.

It may be argued that Burns's language is more incisive, and his perception operating at a deeper level. But can it be denied that the honesty of thought is shared, the scenario to the reader is real that both verses contain that indefinable something which warrant the statement: 'This is what I expect from poetry'?

And yet, behind all the quality of the verse he could produce, there is the feeling that Service is too entertaining, too easy on the ears for him to be regarded as a true poet. His ambition was realised in that his volumes of verse could be read by the ordinary man without any feeling of guilt that something above his comprehension was being attempted. Even when he starts out with heightened language, there is so regularly a line or two which, be it of humour, romance or perhaps related to a manly passion, strikes the reader with the force of a spear thrust and transfixes him, or her, to the verse. Take for example *Naked Grandeur*.

> Have you gazed on naked grandeur where there's nothing else to gaze on,
> Set pieces and drop-curtain scenes galore,
> Big mountains heaved to heaven, which the blinding sunsets blaze on,
> Black canyons where the rapids rip and roar?–
> ... Have you known the Great White silence, not a snow-gemmed
> twig aquiver
> Eternal truths that shame our soothing lies

Then, after this quite magnificent piece of description of nature in the raw comes the challenge to those with adventure in their veins:

> Have you broken trail on snow-shoes? Mushed your huskies up the river
> Dared the unknown, led the way, and clutched the prize?' –
> – Then hearken to the wild – it's wanting you.

Service's verse is of course not all orientated to the physical and the outdoors. The humorous and the tender have their place. And there is a sentimental streak too, as he regards old friends like his accordion. Women collectively he treats properly, indeed graciously, and if 'The Lady Known as Lou' did perhaps blot her copybook by pinching a miner's poke, many of her kind are made to bring womanly virtues into situations of hardship and callousness. Service had no reputation as a ladies man, and one senses a reverence toward the 'weaker sex' that is at times almost quaint.

Service's links with Scotland were always strong, and occasionally he is tempted into writing with a Scots accent such as in his war poem, *The Twa Jocks*. But it is always accent rather than the old Scots tongue, and designed more to give a whiff of authenticity to the situation than create Scots verse. Even if in his later years his voice could still at times betray his origins, Service must never be seen solely as a Scottish or indeed as a Canadian literary figure.

No doubt many countries have their literary figures who made their reputations outwith their own lands. But it is frequently not recognised how many Scots have done so, not because of the greatness of their pens, such as Sir Walter Scott, but because of their travels. Adam Lindsay Gordon with his stirring 'Bush and horse' poems was to occupy in the latter part of last century a position in Australia akin to that of Service in North America. R.B. Cunninghame Graham with his great tales of the pampas is probably more highly revered in the Argentine today than at home. Bruce Lockhart introduced a generation to the intrigues and affairs of the Balkans. And although established before leaving his own soil, Stevenson's travels in America and then in the South Seas provided that extra glamour a public seeks in its literary figures. His Yukon verse brought Service to the attention of the world. Scotland has been slow to capitalise on the success of one of her sons.

But bearing in mind Service's strong Ayrshire connections there is surprise that Burns, at least on the surface, figures so little as a source of inspiration and affection. Nowhere in his autobiographies does Service refer to reading or carrying a copy of the Scottish bard's works. Indeed, there is hardly a direct reference to Burns in his verse, and where there is, such as in *Poet and Peer*, little depth of knowledge is displayed. If Service could write about Katie Drummond and Stevenson, why, one wonders, did he choose to ignore the more fertile ground provided by Burns?

There is, though, one poem of Services that suggests he knew more about Burns than meets the eye. In his collection *Rhymes of a Rolling Stone* written as his time in the Yukon was coming to an end, there, amongst life in the High North, is a poem with the unexpected title of '?' The poem poses an interesting question about choice of wife. Is it not likely that the inspiration for this poem came from a debate held in the Bachelors Club which was formed by Burns and his brother? There is a Minute of the Bachelors Club meeting, which reads:

> Question for Hallowe'en – November 11 1780. Suppose a young man, bred a farmer, but without any fortune, has it in his power to marry either of two women, the one a girl of large fortune, but neither handsome in person, nor agreeable in conversation but who can manage the household affairs well enough: the other a girl every way agreeable in person, conversation and behaviour, but without any fortune: which of them shall he choose?

In that debate, Burns took the imprudent side. Service in his poem adds morals to the ladies' qualities in the debate, but, unlike Burns, is not prepared to commit himself:

> Now, suppose you must wed, and make no blunder,
> And either would love you, and let her you win her –
> Which of the two would you choose, I wonder,
> The stolid saint or the sparkling sinner?

When one seeks a Scottish literary influence on Service, it must be said that little appears to come from Burns. What Scottish hero-worship there was centred on Stevenson, and that was more because of his travels, life-style, outlook and romanticism rather than on anything else. Service has a blood brother in the man who wrote:

> Still I love to rhyme, and still more, rhyming, to wander
> Far from the commoner way;
> Old-time trills and falls by the brookside still do I ponder,
> Dreaming tomorrow today.

What then are we to make of Service; do we give him the accolade of 'Poet' – which he never sought? To those with one foot in academia there must be recognition that he did write lines which can properly be defined as poetry. But the sheer volume of his output, his insistence that metre and rhyme, story and appeal to the masses should triumph over all else, forces us to accept that his vagabond existence extended to his pen. His reputation will ever be that of observer and recorder, spinner of tales, homespun philosopher and companion on life's dusty road. And let us not worry if he cannot tidily be placed in one box or another.

Luigi Orsini, writing in an Italian magazine in 1920, has provided the answer to those who would deny Service a unique place:

> ... and we should be wrong if we tried to quibble about his poetic style and about the suitability of placing him in a particular poetic school. We should run the risk of playing the part of The Man Who Knew, and the bitter lines of this poem would be fully deserved by us:

> Love smote the Dreamer's lips, and silver clear
> He sang the song so sweet, so tender true,
> That all the market place was thrilled to hear,
> And listened rapt – till came the Man Who Knew,
> Saying: 'His Technique's wrong: he singeth ill,
> Waste not your time!' The Singer's voice was still.

> And then the people roused as if from sleep,
> Crying; 'What care we if it be not Art!
> Hath he not charmed us, made us laugh and weep?
> Come, let us crown him where he sits apart!'

For lines like these, Service truly deserves a garland, and recognition that it is wrong to think of him only in 'Bard Of The Yukon' terms. Let us 'crown him where he sits apart', not because he gave us such singular narrative pieces as *Dan McGrew, Sam McGee* and *The Trail of '98*, but because, in the work he produced in over fifty years of writing, he has given us absolutely unique literary richness.

Service wanted to be remembered for all his works. Writing to a well-wisher from his Monte Carlo home the year before he died, he said:

As to writing, to a pukka penman like myself, born to the job, it comes so easy as to be a natural function. From the start I have never been an amateur but was born to be a Grub Street hack or a blatant best-seller. At eighty-four I write a poem a day to keep boredom away. I have three books in the offing and resent people who only know me by my early work.

To come to grips with Service requires a study of all his works. His vintage years were not confined to his Yukon years. Service knew time had conditioned and matured the flow from his pen. It is our loss if we keep a narrow focus on the man.

From the difficult task of assessing Service's place as a poet follows the simpler task of placing his prose work. Service wrote a total of nine prose books. Three of these were autobiographical in nature, and in four of the others he draws very heavily on his own experiences. *The Trail of '98,* for example, is about the Klondike. *The Pretender* introduces its readers to life in the Latin Quarter, while *Poisoned Paradise* penetrates the glitter of the gaming tables. *The Roughneck* appeared as a result of his Tahiti wanderings. The enthusiast for Service's verse frequently experiences disappointment when settling down for a night with one of his novels. The momentum which so characterises his verse is often missing. True, the plots are good, even very good, but the master of the word and phrase in rhyme becomes at times unexpectedly stilted in prose.

While Service's verse is timeless, must we say that, like John Buchan, his novels expressed their period so forcibly that they have dated? That Hollywood showed such interest in his books is understandable – the plots, the exciting locations, the opportunity to create drama on the screen are gifts to the movie maker. It is the reader transferring his allegiance from verse to novel who experiences the difference. There is a feeling that Service would have liked to write as a Jack London or an Ernest Hemingway. Although at times he professed admiration for such colourful characters he was not of their kind.

The former bank clerk, seldom seen without his high starched collar in the Yukon, was not in the hell-raiser mould. He could find himself in dangerous situations, such as the Parisian underworld or lost on the Yukon trail or under shellfire in no-man's land. But he was not the central figure in scrapes with authority, or at wild parties. He was the loner, not the herd leader, the investigative journalist not the history maker, the observer and recorder, not the doer.

It is not so much his powers of description that let Service down, but rather an inability to sustain excitement in dialogue. For example we have in *The Trail of '98*, this picture of the route to the Klondike:

> The river was mud colour now, swirling in great eddies or convulsed from below with sudden upheavals. Drifting on that oily current one seemed to be quite motionless, and only the gliding banks assured us of progress. The country seemed terrible to me, sinister, guilty, God-forsaken. The river overwhelmed me. Sometimes it was a stream of blood, running into the eye of the setting sun, beautiful yet weird and menacing. Islands waded in it greenly.

And then comes the stilted (perhaps dated) conversation:

> I thought for a while ere I went on.
>
> 'You cared for your grandfather; you gave him your whole heart, a love full of self-sacrifice, of renunciation. Now he is gone you will love again, but the next will be to the last as wine is to water. And the day will come when you will love grandly. Yours will be a great, consuming passion that knows no limit, no assuagement. It will be your glory and your shame. For him will your friends be foes, your light darkness. You will go through fire and water for your beloved's sake; your parched lips will call his name, your frail hands cling to him in the shadow of death.'

The strength of his writing is so often his inside knowledge of his subject, as in the Casino scene from *The Poisoned Paradise*.

Every time she played Mr. Gimp would play on the opposite chance. But while the honey-coloured beauty threw on heaps of plaques, now rising to a rose, now dropping to azure, Mr. Gimp played only a modest Louis. Behind his hand he whispered to Hugh:

'This is the best system of all. It's known as 'playing the corpse.' You get opposite a big player and play the contrary. When they have to make a progression, you win on all its terms. It goes without saying they're dead ones from the start. The Casino will get their money. You're playing on the side of the Casino, that's all. And while the Casino is taking big risks, you are taking small ones. 'Playing the corpse,' – it's the only sure business I know. It's a shame to take the money'

When Hugh returned late in the afternoon the beautiful American was still playing, and opposite her, methodically putting on his single louts was the pertinacious Mr. Gimp.

For those who like their gambling encounters to be less practical, Service kindly said it in verse:

The plunging players pack the tables,
Beneath the bunched electric's glare;
The tumult is the Tower of Babel's,
As strong as Camembert the air.
The counters click, the balls are spinning,
The number eight three times repeats –
There was a fortune for my winning: –

Those interested in a more detailed study of Service as a novelist should seek out the late Professor Carl Klinck's book. It is out of print now, but a good library should have a copy.

Service's autobiographical works offer a different style from his novels. One senses in them the adoption of a more relaxed mode; the pleasure associated with reminiscing is present. The worries and failures are paraded, but the feelings and philosophies are in keeping with what has been encountered in his verse, so that overall one feels closer to the man. No doubt the assurance of age is reflected in *Ploughman of the Moon* and *Harper of Heaven*, his two records of his life. These two books were published in the 1940s, some twenty years after his last novel, *The House of Fear*, came out. But this same easy and endearingly intimate, almost confidential style can be noted in what to many is their favourite Service book. *In Why Not Grow Young*, Service rambles on about health, diet and himself, proffering advice and recalling incidents, joyously harking back to his days of great physical fitness, nostalgically remembering the joys of nicotine and alcohol. It was perhaps a book written ahead of its time, and if published today in our less puritanical society, would undoubtedly be represented on more bookshelves; humour and good advice are excellent bedfellows:

> Fifty is the age of reform, and lucky is he on whom it is not imposed. There is no virtue in reform. It's a confession of failure, of transgression. But transgression and reformation are all part of a rich and balanced life. The man who has no need to reform has never lived. Believing we all should sow our wild oats, I cannot be condemned as a moralist. Save your money, stick to your job, marry early and settle down ... what pernicious advice! Perhaps good advice has ruined more men than bad. And to marry early is to court calamity. People of nearly the same age should never marry, for the woman will be old when the man is still young, and then the trouble will begin. Let no man marry till he is secure in life, and let him be at least ten years older than his wife.

It is not unusual for those writing their autobiographies to keep a few secrets, to miss out a few items, to lay a few false trails. Service has a right to his own reservations, but his relationship with 'Dream Haven' has puzzled many. Had he wanted to keep his address or whereabouts a secret, it would have been easy for him to ignore its location entirely in his autobiography. Instead, he tempts us on to the trail before taking steps to cover his tracks. He describes Dream Haven as a cottage, (in an interview he even referred to it as a shrimping shack) and although indicating its proximity to Saint Malo, never mentions the small town in which it is situated. His Canadian trail has been so successfully smothered that most Canadians are not aware that his years in British Columbia were spent on Vancouver Island. He gives little away about his family and friends. The preciousness of those personal relationships is not be be enlarged upon: private lives are to remain private. And, significantly, he discloses remarkably little about himself that would cast him in the mould of one of his own characters.

People in Lancieux love to tell the story of how when canoeing one day he saved a young boy from drowning. Having been dragged ashore and with the water pumped from him, the boy then started to cry because he had lost his shoes in the water and would not be pacified until Service returned to the spot of the near-tragedy, and after some under-water swimming, rescued the missing footwear.

Ploughman of the Moon starts with Service at the age of five. He has surprisingly little to say about his parents, although his father's Ayrshire connections are evident through the young Robert's stay in Kilwinning. It has been left to others to claim that Service's mother, Emily Parker, was English and came from a wealthy cotton factory-owning family in Preston, Lancashire. But the Preston directories of the 1870s provide no supporting evidence. That she inherited wealth is not doubted. The interesting point is that 'Parker' is an Ayrshire name, and many Parkers were connected with textiles and weaving.

But Service had incredibly little interest in his relations. 'Ancestry,' he once said, 'is not my bug,' and people of the name Service writing to him seeking to establish a relationship would find him polite, but unhelpful. Whether or not his maternal grandfather also had Ayrshire origins has yet to be discovered. Was Service happy once again to sit back allowing others to follow a false trail?

But one thing *Ploughman of the Moon* does have is a superb beginning, designed to make the reader hungry for more:

'Please, Aunt Jeannie, can I go and look at the hens?'
    Over her spectacles my aunt gazed at me suspiciously. 'Whit fur, Rubbert Wullie, do you want to look at the hens?'
    'I don't know whit fur, I just want to look at them.'
    'Ye'd be faur better lookin' at yer bonnie Bible. Don't ye like yer wee Bible?'
    ' Ay, but I like the hens better.'

No reference to Service's prose would be complete without mention of his *Bath-Tub Ballads*. Service was an accomplished musician. As we have noted, in addition to playing the accordion and concertina, he played the banjo and guitar and could usefully vamp on the piano. *Bath Tub Ballads* are a selection of, in the main, pretty awful songs, fit only to be sung in a bathroom. But two of them will be with us for a long time yet. Canadian Heritage Songs of Calgary in its *Canada – A Land and its Songs*, which associates the various Provinces with their music, uses Service's *When The Ice Worm Nests Again* as the appropriate Yukon anthem. And not a few Scots still find the robustness of *Going Back to Scotland*, with its phonetic 'All change for Auchtermuchty, Eccelfechan and Mulguy' worthy of a chorus or two on the appropriate celebration. The tunes for these ditties are good. It is a pity Service did not seek to share this talent of his with a wider audience.

Acknowledgements

MY MAIN EXPRESSION OF THANKS for help given with this book must go to Madame Iris Service Davies, the daughter of the Bard. Not only because she has read and corrected my proofs, enlarged on events, provided photographs of her father, and given me permission to quote so liberally from his books, but because of her confidence that the book would be worthy of Robert Service. The encouragement and friendship given to me by this most gracious lady means more than I can say. And let my thoughts not stray from France without expressing gratitude to Mademoiselle Marie Dagorne who again not only provided me with information, but with the greatest kindness helped my enquiries in so many ways. To Monsieur le Maire de Lancieux I also acknowledge my debt.

The Universities of Glasgow and British Columbia provided me with documents. Amongst libraries, I must single out the Mitchell in Glasgow, Kilwinning Public Library, Ayrshire, and Preston District Library for special efforts on my behalf. In Canada, especially helpful have been the Public Archives in Ottawa, Dawson Museum and Historical Society, The Yukon Department of Tourism, Heritage and Cultural Resources, the Yukon Library and Archives, British Columbia Provincial Archives, and the Calgary City Library. My visits to the Yukon Library and Archives in Whitehorse were all the more enjoyable because of the three Scots members of staff determined to leave no stone unturned on my behalf.

That famous chronicle of the North, *The Whitehorse Star*, came to my aid, and I am also obliged to the Anglican Church in Whitehorse. Duncan Chamber of Commerce provided assistance and I am overwhelmingly in the debt of Jack Fleetwood of Cowichan Station with his unsurpassed knowledge of Robert Service's life while on Vancouver Island. Coming nearer home, I must make mention of the help given by Mrs Anne Millar of Bearsden and Mr A.R. Craig, Headmaster of Hillhead High School, Glasgow. And let me add here the names of two books which have helped me enormously in my study of Robert Service. They are *I Married the Klondike* by Laura Berton (Hutchison) and *Klondike* by Pierre Berton (W.H. Allen).

The above formal acknowledgements leave out the numerous people in North America and at home, who, over the years, have supplied me with articles and added bits and pieces to my knowledge about Robert Service. I trust they know I have always been appreciative of their help.

In this second edition I acknowledge the additional photographs made available to me by Madame Iris Service Davies and Mademoiselle Marie Dagorne of Lancieux. I am also grateful to Peter Mitham, now residing in the Province of New Brunswick, for access to his bibliographical work.

Scanning the Years

1874 Robert William Service born in Preston, Lancashire, on 16th January.

1878 Takes up residence with Grandfather and three maiden aunts in Kilwinning, Ayrshire.

1879 Attends Parish school, Kilwinning.

1880 Record of first verse on sixth birthday.

1883 Joins family in Glasgow. Attends Church Street Primary School.

1885 Attends Hillhead High School.

1888 Enters employ of Commercial Bank of Scotland.

1896 Emigrates to Vancouver Island.

1897 The wandering and unsettled years. The Western States and British Columbia.

1903 Joins the Canadian Bank of Commerce in Victoria.

1904 Posted by Bank first to Kamloops, BC, then Whitehorse in the Yukon Territory. The Service family move to Canada.

1905 Starts to versify seriously.

1907 Publication of *Songs of a Sourdough*.

1908 Posted by Bank to Dawson, Yukon Territory.

1909 *Ballads of a Cheechako* published. Resigns from the Canadian Bank of Commerce.

1910 *The Trail of '98* published. Visits New York, Southern States and Cuba. Winters with family in Alberta.

1911 Undertakes remarkable return journey of nearly two thousand miles to Dawson via the Athabaska River, Great Slave, Fort Simpson and Fort Macpherson, manhandles canoe over 'Great Divide' and returns to Dawson from the North view Bell River and the Porcupine.

1912 *Rhymes of a Rolling Stone* published. Accepts the position of war correspondent in the Balkans offered by the *Toronto Star*. Experiences the horrors of war, clashes with authority. Journeys to Budapest and Vienna.

1913   Arrives in Paris where he retained a base for fifteen years. Moves in newspaper, literary and art circles. Explores Brittany, buys 'Dream Haven' and marries Germaine Bourgoin.

1914   Novel *The Pretender* published. Turned down by army on medical grounds.

1915   War Correspondent for *Toronto Star*. Joins American Ambulance Unit.

1916   Invalidated out of Unit. *Rhymes of a Red Cross Man* published.

1917   Becomes father of twin girls. Accepts reporting position with Canadian Expeditionary Force.

1918   Death of daughter, Doris. Returns to French life.

1921   Starts his explorations of the seamier places of Paris. *Ballads of a Bohemian* published. Visits Hollywood. Sets out for the South Seas, walks round Tahiti.

1922   Novel *The Poisoned Paradise* published. Made into a film.

1923   Novel *The Roughneck* published.

1924   *The Roughneck* made into a film.

1926   Novel *The Master of the Microbe* published. Suffers from athlete's heart. Starts his visits to spa at Royat.

1927   Novel *The House of Fear* published.

1928   Autobiographical book *Why Not Grow Young?* published.

1929   Takes up residence and adopts a quiet life on the Rivera.

1930   *Collected Verse* published.

1933   *Complete Poems* published.

1938   Travels to Russia.

1939   Publication of a book of songs, *Bath-Tub Ballads*. Returns to Russia. After Moscow takes boat down the Volga, Rostov. Drives across Caucasus Mountains to Black Sea. On return journey home gets caught up in the war in Poland. Arrives home via Estonia and Sweden.

1940   Forced by advance of German troops to flee 'Dream Haven'. Makes for England. Crosses Atlantic eventually settling in Hollywood. *Bar Room Ballads* published.

-1945   The war years. Gives talks, broadcasts. Given a one-line part in a film with John Wayne and Marlene Dietrich. Entertain troops.

Writes first volume of his autobiography, *Ploughman of the Moon*. Returns to Nice.

1947   Spends much time in Dream Haven. Writes second volume of autobiography, *Harper of Heaven*. Moves his Riviera home from Nice to Monte Carlo.

1948   Attends 'Sourdoughs' celebration in Vancouver marking fiftieth anniversary of the '98 trail.

1949   Leads a quiet existence but writes unceasingly. Publications include:
Songs of a Sun Lover – 1949
Rhymes of a Roughneck – 1950
Lyrics of a Lowbrow – 1951
Rhymes of a Rebel – 1952
Songs for my Supper – 1953
Carols of an Old Codger – 1954
Later Collected Verse – 1954
More Collected Verse – 1955
Rhymes for my Rags – 1956

1958   Robert Service dies in Lancieux in September 1958.

Some other books published by **LUATH** PRESS

MUSIC AND DANCE

Highland Balls and Village Halls
GW Lockhart
ISBN 0 946487 12 X PBK £6.95

Acknowledged as a classic in Scottish danc-ing circles throughout the world. Anecdotes, Scottish history, dress and dance steps are all included in this

'delightful little book, full of interest... both a personal account and an understanding look at the making of traditions.'
NEW ZEALAND SCOTTISH COUN-TRY DANCES MAGAZINE

'A delightful survey of Scottish dancing and custom. Informative, concise and opinion-ated, it guides the reader across the history and geography of country dance and ends by detailing the 12 dances every Scot should know – the most famous being the Eightsome Reel, "the greatest longest, row-diest, most diabolically executed of all the Scottish country dances".' THE HERALD

'A pot-pourri of every facet of Scottish country dancing. It will bring back memo-ries of petronella turns and poussettes and make you eager to take part in a Broun's reel or a dashing white sergeant!'
DUNDEE COURIER AND ADVERTISER

'An excellent an very readable insight into the traditions and customs of Scottish country dancing. The author takes us on a tour from his own early days jigging in the village hall to the characters and traditions that have made our own brand of dance popular throughout the world.' SUNDAY POST

Fiddles & Folk: A celebration of the re-emergence of Scotland's musical heritage
GW Lockhart
ISBN 0 946487 38 3 PBK £7.95

In *Fiddles & Folk*, his companion volume to *Highland Balls and Village Halls*, Wallace Lockhart meets up with many of the people who have created the renaissance of Scot-land's music at home and overseas.

From Dougie MacLean, Hamish Henderson, the Battlefield Band, the Whistlebinkies, the Scottish Fiddle Orchestra, the McCalmans and many more come the stories that break down the musical barriers between Scotland's past and present, and between the diverse musical forms which have woven together to create the dynamism of the music today.

'I have tried to avoid a formal approach to Scottish music as it affects those of us with our musical heritage coursing through our veins. The picture I have sought is one of many brush strokes, looking at how some individuals have come to the fore, examin-ing their music, lives, thoughts, even philosophies...' WALLACE LOCKHART

' "I never had a narrow, woolly-jumper, fingers stuck in the ear approach to music. We have a musical heritage here that is the envy of the rest of the world. Most coun-tries just can't compete," he [Ian Green, Greentrax] says. And as young Scots tire of Oasis and Blur, they will realise that there is a wealth of young Scottish music on their doorstep just waiting to be discov-ered.' THE SCOTSMAN

For anyone whose heart lifts at the sound of fiddle or pipes, this book takes you on a delightful journey, full of humour and respect, in the company of some of the performers who have taken Scotland's music around the world and come back enriched.

LUATH PRESS LIMITED

LUATH GRAPHICS

Old Scotland New Scotland

Jeff Fallow

ISBN 0 946487 40 5 PBK £6.99

'Together we can build a new Scotland based on Labour's values.' DONALD DEWAR, Party Political Broadcast

'Despite the efforts of decent Mr Dewar, the voters may yet conclude they are looking at the same old hacks in brand new suits.' IAN BELL, *The Independent*

'At times like this you suddenly realise how dangerous the neglect of Scottish history in our schools and universities may turn out to be.' MICHAEL FRY, *The Herald*

'...one of the things I hope will go is our chip on the shoulder about the English... The SNP has a huge responsibility to articulate Scottish independence in a way that is pro-Scottish and not anti-English.' ALEX SALMOND, *The Scotsman*

Scottish politics have never been more exciting. In *old Scotland new Scotland* Jeff Fallow takes us on a graphic voyage through Scotland's turbulent history, from earliest times through to the present day and beyond. This fast-track guide is the quick way to learn what your history teacher didn't tell you, essential reading for all who seek an understanding of Scotland and its history.

Eschewing the romanticisation of his country's past, Fallow offers a new perspective on an old nation. 'Too many people associate Scottish history with tartan trivia or outworn romantic myth. This book aims to blast that stubborn idea.' JEFF FALLOW

BIOGRAPHY

Tobermory Teuchter: A first-hand account of life on Mull in the early years of the 20th century

Peter Macnab

ISBN 0 946487 41 3 PBK £7.99

Peter Macnab was reared on Mull, as was his father, and his grandfather before him. In this book he provides a revealing account of life on Mull during the first quarter of the 20th century, focusing especially on the years of World War I. This enthralling social history of the island is set against Peter Macnab's early years as son of the governor of the Mull Poorhouse, one of the last in the Hebrides, and is illustrated throughout by photo-graphs from his exceptional collec-tion. Peter Macnab's 'fisherman's yarns' and other personal reminis-cences are told delightfully by a born storyteller.

This latest work from the author of a range of books about the island, including the standard study of Mull and Iona, reveals his unparalleled knowledge of and deep feeling for Mull and its people. After his long career with the Clydesdale Bank, first in Tobermory and later on the mainland, Peter, now 94, remains a teuchter at heart, proud of his island heritage.

'Peter Macnab is a man of words who doesnit mince his words - not where his beloved Mull is concerned. 'I will never forget some of the inmates of the poorhouse,' says Peter. 'Some of them were actually victims of the later Clearances. It was history at first hand, and there was no romance about it'. But Peter Macnab sees little creative point in crying over ancient injustices. For him the task is to help Mull in this century and beyond.'
SCOTS MAGAZINE, May 1998

Bare Feet and Tackety Boots

Archie Cameron

ISBN 0 946487 17 0 PBK £7.95

The island of Rum before the First World War was the playground of its rich absentee landowner. A survivor of life a century gone tells his story. Factors and schoolmasters, midges and poaching, deer, ducks and Mac-Brayne's steamers: here social history and personal anecdote create a record of a way of life gone not long ago but already almost forgotten. This is the story the gentry couldn't tell.

'*This book is an important piece of social history, for it gives an insight into how the other half lived in an era the likes of which will never be seen again*'
FORTHRIGHT MAGAZINE

'*The authentic breath of the pawky, country-wise estate employee.*'
THE OBSERVER

'*Well observed and detailed account of island life in the early years of this century*' THE SCOTS MAGAZINE
'*A very good read with the capacity to make the reader chuckle. A very talented writer.*' STORNOWAY GAZETTE

Come Dungeons Dark

John Taylor Caldwell

ISBN 0 946487 19 7 PBK £6.95

Glasgow anarchist Guy Aldred died with 10p in his pocket in 1963 claiming there was better company in Barlinnie Prison than in the Corridors of Power. 'The Red Scourge' is remembered here by one who worked with him and spent 27 years as part of his turbulent household, sparring with Lenin, Sylvia Pankhurst and others as he struggled for freedom for his beloved fellow-man.

'*The welcome and long-awaited biography of... one of this country's most prolific radical propagandists... Crank or visionary?... whatever the verdict, the Glasgow anarchist has finally been given a fitting memorial.*'
THE SCOTSMAN

LUATH GUIDES TO SCOTLAND

These guides are not your traditional where-to-stay and what-to-eat books. They are companions in the rucksack or car seat, providing the discerning traveller with a blend of fiery opinion and moving description. Here you will find '*that curious pastiche of myths and legend and history that the Scots use to describe their heritage... what battle happened in which glen between which clans; where the Picts sacrificed bulls as recently as the 17th century... A lively counterpoint to the more standard, detached guidebook... Intriguing.*'
THE WASHINGTON POST

These are perfect guides for the discerning visitor or resident to keep close by for reading again and again, written by authors who invite you to share their intimate knowledge and love of the areas covered.

Highways and Byways in Mull and Iona

Peter Macnab

ISBN 0 946487 16 2 PBK £4.25

'The Isle of Mull is of Isles the fairest,
Of ocean's gems 'tis the first and rarest.'
So a local poet described it a hundred years ago, and this recently revised guide to Mull and sacred Iona, the most accessible islands of the Inner Hebrides, takes the reader on a delightful tour of these rare ocean gems, travelling with a native whose unparal-

leled knowledge and deep feeling for the area unlock the byways of the islands in all their natural beauty.

South West Scotland

Tom Atkinson

ISBN 0 946487 04 9 PBK £4.95

This descriptive guide to the magical country of Robert Burns covers Kyle, Carrick, Galloway, Dumfries-shire, Kirkcudbrightshire and Wigtownshire. Hills, unknown moors and unspoiled beaches grace a land steeped in history and legend and portrayed with affection and deep delight.

An essential book for the visitor who yearns to feel at home in this land of peace and grandeur.

The Lonely Lands

Tom Atkinson

ISBN 0 946487 10 3 PBK £4.95

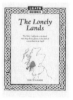

A guide to Inveraray, Glencoe, Loch Awe, Loch Lomond, Cowal, the Kyles of Bute and all of central Argyll written with insight, sympathy and loving detail. Once Atkinson has taken you there, these lands can never feel lonely. 'I have sought to make the complex simple, the beautiful accessible and the strange familiar,' he writes, and indeed he brings to the land a knowledge and affection only accessible to someone with intimate knowledge of the area.

A must for travellers and natives who want to delve beneath the surface.

'Highly personal and somewhat quirky... steeped in the lore of Scotland.'
THE WASHINGTON POST

The Empty Lands

Tom Atkinson

ISBN 0 946487 13 8 PBK £4.95

The Highlands of Scotland from Ullapool to Bettyhill and Bonar Bridge to John O'Groats are landscapes of myth and legend, 'empty of people, but of nothing else that brings delight to any tired soul,' writes Atkinson. This highly personal guide describes Highland history and landscape with love, compassion and above all sheer magic. Essential reading for anyone who has dreamed of the Highlands.

Roads to the Isles

Tom Atkinson

ISBN 0 946487 01 4 PBK £4.95

Ardnamurchan, Morvern, Morar, Moidart and the west coast to Ulla-pool are included in this guide to the Far West and Far North of Scotland. An unspoiled land of mountains, lochs and silver sands is brought to the walker's toe-tips (and to the reader's fingertips) in this stark, serene and evocative account of town, country and legend.

For any visitor to this Highland wonderland, Queen Victoria's favourite place on earth.

FICTION
The Bannockburn Years

William Scott

ISBN 0 946487 34 0 PBK £7.95

A present day Edinburgh solicitor stumbles across reference to a document of value to the Nation State of Scotland. He tracks down the document on the

Isle of Bute, a document which probes the real 'quaestiones' about nationhood and national identity. The document ends up being published, but is it authentic and does it matter? Almost 700 years on, these 'quaestiones' are still worth asking.

Written with pace and passion, William Scott has devised an intriguing vehicle to open up new ways of looking at the future of Scotland and its people. He presents an alternative inter-pretation of how the Battle of Bannockburn was fought, and through the Bannatyne manuscript he draws the reader into the minds of those involved.

Winner of the 1997 Constable Trophy, the premier award in Scotland for an unpublished novel, this book offers new insights to both the academic and the general reader which are sure to provoke further discussion and debate.

'A brilliant storyteller. I shall expect to see your name writ large hereafter.'
NIGEL TRANTER, October 1997.

'... a compulsive read.' PH Scott, THE SCOTSMAN

The Great Melnikov

Hugh MacLachlan
ISBN 0 946487 42 1 PBK £7.95

A well crafted, gripping novel, written in a style reminiscent of John Buchan and set in London and the Scottish Highlands during the First World War, The Great Melnikov is a dark tale of double-cross and deception. We first meet Melnikov, one-time star of the German

circus, languishing as a down-and-out in Trafalgar Square. He soon finds himself drawn into a tortuous web of intrigue. He is a complex man whose personal struggle with alcoholism is an inner drama which parallels the tense twists and turns as a spy mystery unfolds. Melnikov's options are narrowing. The circle of threat is closing. Will Melnikov outwit the sinister enemy spy network? Can he summon the will and the wit to survive?

Hugh MacLachlan, in his first full length novel, demonstrates an undoubted ability to tell a good story well. His earlier stories have been broadcast on Radio Scotland, and he has the rare distinction of being short-listed for the Macallan/Scotland on Sunday Short Story Competition two years in succession.

FOLKLORE

The Supernatural Highlands

Francis Thompson
ISBN 0 946487 31 6 PBK £8.99

An authoritative exploration of the otherworld of the Highlander, happenings and beings hitherto thought to be outwith the ordinary forces of nature. A simple introduction to the way of life of rural Highland and Island communities, this new edition weaves a path through second sight, the evil eye, witchcraft, ghosts, fairies and other supernatural beings, offering new sight-lines on areas of belief once dismissed as folklore and superstition.

Tall Tales from an Island

Peter Macnab

ISBN 0 946487 07 3 PBK £8.99

Peter Macnab was born and reared on Mull. He heard many of these tales as a lad, and others he has listened to in later years. There are humorous tales, grim tales, witty tales, tales of witchcraft, tales of love, tales of heroism, tales of treachery, historical tales and tales of yesteryear.

A popular lecturer, broadcaster and writer, Peter Macnab is the author of a number of books and articles about Mull, the island he knows so intimately and loves so much. As he himself puts it in his introduction to this book 'I am of the unswerving opinion that nowhere else in the world will you find a better way of life, nor a finer people with whom to share it.'

'All islands, it seems, have a rich store of characters whose stories represent a kind of sub-culture without which island life would be that much poorer. Macnab has succeeded in giving the retelling of the stories a special Mull flavour, so much so that one can visualise the storytellers sitting on a bench outside the house with a few cronies, puffing on their pipes and listening with nodding approval.' WEST HIGHLAND FREE PRESS

NATURAL SCOTLAND

Rum: Nature's Island

Magnus Magnusson

ISBN 0 946487 32 4 £7.95 PBK

Rum: Nature's Island is the fascinating story of a Hebridean island from the earliest times through to the Clearances and its period as the sporting playground of a Lancashire industrial magnate, and

on to its rebirth as a National Nature Reserve, a model for the active ecological management of Scotland's wild places.

Thoroughly researched and written in a lively accessible style, the book includes comprehensive coverage of the island's geology, animals and plants, and people, with a special chapter on the Edwardian extravaganza of Kinloch Castle. There is practical information for visitors to what was once known as 'the Forbidden Isle'; the book provides details of bothy and other accommodation, walks and nature trails. It closes with a positive vision for the island's future: biologically diverse, economically dynamic and ecologically sustainable.

Rum: Nature's Island is published in co-operation with Scottish Natural Heritage (of which Magnus Magnusson is Chairman) to mark the 40th anniversary of the acquisition of Rum by its predecessor, The Nature Conservancy.

Wild Scotland: The essential guide to finding the best of natural Scotland

James McCarthy

Photography by Laurie Campbell

ISBN 0 946487 37 5 PBK £7.50

With a foreword by Magnus Magnusson and striking colour photographs by Laurie Campbell, this is the essential up-to-date guide to viewing wildlife in Scotland for the visitor and resident alike. It provides a fascinating overview of the country's plants, animals, bird and marine life against the background of their typical natural settings, as an introduction to the vivid descriptions of the most accessible localities, linked to clear regional maps. A unique feature is the focus on 'green tourism' and sustainable visitor use of the countryside, contributed by Duncan Bryden, manager of the Scottish Tourist Board's Tourism and the Environment Task Force. Important practical information on access and the best times of year for viewing sites makes this an indispensable and user-friendly travelling companion to anyone interested in exploring Scotland's remarkable natural heritage.

James McCarthy is former Deputy Director for Scotland of the Nature Conservancy Council, and now a Board Member of Scottish Natural Heritage and Chairman of the Environmental Youth Work National Development Project Scotland.

Scotland Land and People
An Inhabited Solitude

James McCarthy

ISBN 0 946487 57 X PBK £7.99

'Scotland is the country above all others that I have seen, in which a man of imagination may carve out his own pleasures; there are so many inhabited solitudes.'
DOROTHY WORDSWORTH, in her journal of August 1803

An informed and thought-provoking profile of Scotland's unique land-scapes and the impact of humans on what we see now and in the future. James McCarthy leads us through the many aspects of the land and the people who inhabit it: natural Scotland; the rocks beneath; land ownership; the use of resources; people and place; conserving Scotland's heritage and much more.

Written in a highly readable style, this concise volume offers an under-stand-ing of the land as a whole. Emphasising the uniqueness of the Scottish environment, the author explores the links between this and other aspects of our culture as a key element in rediscovering a modern sense of the Scottish identity and perception of nationhood.

'This book provides an engaging introduction to the mysteries of Scotland's people and landscapes. Difficult concepts are described in simple terms, providing the interested Scot or tourist with an invaluable overview of the country... It fills an important niche which, to my knowledge, is filled by no other publications.'

BETSY KING, Chief Executive, Scottish Environmental Education Council.

The Highland Geology Trail

John L Roberts

ISBN 0946487 36 7   PBK £4.99

Where can you find the oldest rocks in Europe?
Where can you see ancient hills around 800 million years old?
How do you tell whether a valley was carved out by a glacier, not a river?
What are the Fucoid Beds?
Where do you find rocks folded like putty?
How did great masses of rock pile up like snow in front of a snow-plough?
When did volcanoes spew lava and ash to form Skye, Mull and Rum?
Where can you find fossils on Skye?

'...a lucid introduction to the geological record in general, a jargon-free exposition of the regional background, and a series of descriptions of specific localities of geological interest on a "trail" around the highlands.

Having checked out the local references on the ground, I can vouch for their accuracy and look forward to investigating farther afield, informed by this guide.

Great care has been taken to explain specific terms as they occur and, in so doing, John

Roberts has created a resource of great value which is eminently usable by anyone with an interest in the outdoors...the best bargain you are likely to get as a geology book in the foreseeable future.'
Jim Johnston, PRESS AND JOURNAL

WALK WITH LUATH

Mountain Days & Bothy Nights

Dave Brown and Ian Mitchell

ISBN 0 946487 15 4 PBK £7.50

Acknowledged as a classic of mountain writing still in demand ten years after its first publication, this book takes you into the bothies, howffs and dosses on the Scottish hills. Fishgut Mac, Desperate Dan and Stumpy the Big Yin stalk hill and public house, evading gamekeepers and Royalty with a camaraderie which was the trademark of Scots hillwalking in the early days.

'The fun element comes through... how innocent the social polemic seems in our nastier world of today... the book for the rucksack this year.'
Hamish Brown, SCOTTISH MOUNTAINEERING CLUB JOURNAL

The Joy of Hillwalking

Ralph Storer

ISBN 0 946487 28 6 PBK £7.50

Apart, perhaps, from the joy of sex, the joy of hillwalking brings more pleasure to more people than any other form of human activity.

'Alps, America, Scandinavia, you name it – Storer's been there, so why the hell shouldn't he bring all these various and varied places into his observations... [He] even admits to losing

his virginity after a day on the Aggy Ridge... Well worth its place alongside Storer's earlier works.' TAC

Scotland's Mountains before the Mountaineers

Ian Mitchell

ISBN 0 946487 39 1 PBK £9.99

In this ground-breaking book, Ian Mitchell tells the story of explorations and ascents in the Scottish Highlands in the days before mountaineering became a popular sport – when bandits, Jacobites, poachers and illicit distillers traditionally used the mountains as sanctuary. The book also gives a detailed account of the map makers, road builders, geologists, astronomers and naturalists, many of whom ascended hitherto untrodden summits while working in the Scottish Highlands.

Scotland's Mountains before the Mountaineers is divided into four Highland regions, with a map of each region showing key summits. While not designed primarily as a guide, it will be a useful handbook for walkers and climbers. Based on a wealth of new research, this book offers a fresh perspective that will fascinate climbers and mountaineers and everyone interested in the history of mountaineering, cartography, the evolution of landscape and the social history of the Scottish Highlands.

LUATH WALKING GUIDES

The highly respected and continually updated guides to the Cairngorms.

'Particularly good on local wildlife and how to see it' THE COUNTRYMAN

Walks in the Cairngorms

Ernest Cross

ISBN 0 946487 09 X PBK £3.95

This selection of walks celebrates the rare birds, animals, plants and geological wonders of a region often believed difficult to penetrate on foot. Nothing is difficult with this guide in your pocket, as Cross gives a choice for every walker, and includes valuable tips on mountain safety and weather advice.

Ideal for walkers of all ages and skiers waiting for snowier skies.

Short Walks in the Cairngorms

Ernest Cross

ISBN 0 946487 23 5 PBK £3.95

Cross wrote this volume after overhearing a walker remark that there were no short walks for lazy ramblers in the Cairngorm region. Here is the answer: rambles through scenic woods with a welcoming pub at the end, birdwatching hints, glacier holes, or for the fit and ambitious, scrambles up hills to admire vistas of glorious scenery. Wildlife in the Cairngorms is unequalled elsewhere in Britain, and here it is brought to the binoculars of any walker who treads quietly and with respect.

SPORT

Over the Top with the Tartan Army (Active Service 1992-97)

Andrew McArthur

ISBN 0 946487 45 6 PBK £7.99

Scotland has wit-nessed the growth of a new and curious military phenomenon

– grown men bedecked in tartan yomping across the globe, hell-bent on benevolence and ritualistic bevvy-ing. What noble cause does this famous army serve? Why, football of course!

Taking us on an erratic world tour, McArthur gives a frighteningly funny insider's eye view of active service with the Tartan Army - the madcap antics of Scotland's travelling support in the '90s, written from the inside, covering campaigns and skirmishes from Euro '92 up to the qualifying drama for France '98 in places as diverse as Russia, the Faroes, Belarus, Sweden, Monte Carlo, Estonia, Latvia, USA and Finland.

This book is a must for any football fan who likes a good laugh.

'I commend this book to all football supporters'. Graham Spiers, SCOTLAND ON SUNDAY

'In wishing Andy McArthur all the best with this publication, I do hope he will be in a position to produce a sequel after our participation in the World Cup in France'. CRAIG BROWN, Scotland Team Coach

All royalties on sales of the book are going to Scottish charities.

Ski & Snowboard Scotland

Hilary Parke

ISBN 0 946487 35 9 PBK £6.99

Snowsports in Scotland are still a secret treasure. There's no need to go abroad when there's such an exciting variety of terrain right here on your doorstep. You just need to know what to look for. *Ski & Snowboard Scotland* is aimed at maximising the time you have available so that

the hours you spend on the snow are memorable for all the right reasons. This fun and informative book guides you over the slopes of Scotland, giving you the inside track on all the major ski centres. There are chapters ranging from how to get there to the impact of snowsports on the environment.

'Reading the book brought back many happy memories of my early training days at the dry slope in Edinburgh and of many brilliant weekends in the Cairngorms.'

EMMA CARRICK-ANDERSON, from her foreword, written in the US, during a break in training for her first World Cup as a member of the British Alpine Ski Team.

SOCIAL HISTORY

Notes from the North
incorporating a Brief History of
the Scots and the English
Emma Wood
ISBN 0 946487 46 4 PBK £8.99

Notes on being English
Notes on being in Scotland
Learning from a shared past

Is it time to recognise that the border between Scotland and England is the dividing line between very different cultures?

As the Scottish nation begins to set its own agenda, will it decide to consign its sense of grievance against England to the dustbin of history?

Will a fresh approach heal these ancient 'sibling rivalries'?

How does a study of Scottish history help to clarify the roots of Scottish-English antagonism?

Does an English 'white settler' have a right to contribute to the debate?

Will the empowering of the citizens of Scotland take us all, Scots and English, towards mutual tolerance and understanding?

Sickened by the English jingoism that surfaced in rampant form during the 1982 Falklands War, Emma Wood started to dream of moving from her home in East Anglia to the Highlands of Scotland. She felt increasingly frustrated and marginalised as Thatcherism got a grip on the southern English psyche. The Scots she met on frequent holidays in the Highlands had no truck with Thatcherism, and she felt at home with grass-roots Scottish anti-authoritarianism. The decision was made. She uprooted and headed for a new life in the north of Scotland.

'An intelligent and perceptive book... calm, reflective, witty and sensitive. It should certainly be read by all English visitors to Scotland, be they tourists or incomers. And it should certainly be read by all Scots concerned about what kind of nation we live in. They might learn something about themselves.'
THE HERALD

'... her enlightenment is evident on every page of this perceptive, provocative book.'
MAIL ON SUNDAY

A Word for Scotland

Jack Campbell
with a foreword by Magnus Magnusson
ISBN 0 946487 48 0 PBK £12.99

'A word for Scotland' was Lord Beaverbrook's hope when he founded the *Scottish Daily Express*. That word for Scotland quickly became, and was for many years, the national newspaper of Scotland.

The pages of *A Word For Scotland* exude warmth and a wry sense of humour. Jack Campbell takes us behind the scenes to meet the larger-than-life characters and ordinary people who made and recorded the stories. Here we hear the stories behind the stories that hit the headlines in this great yarn of journalism in action.

It would be true to say 'all life is here'. From the Cheapside Street fire of which cost the lives of 19 Glasgow firemen, to the theft of the Stone of Destiny, to the lurid exploits of serial killer Peter Manuel, to encounters with world boxing champions Benny Lynch and Cassius Clay - this book offers telling glimpses of the characters, events, joy and tragedy which make up Scotland's story in the 20th century.

'As a rookie reporter you were proud to work on it and proud to be part of it - it was fine newspaper right at the heartbeat of Scotland.'

RONALD NEIL, Chief Executive of BBC Production, and a reporter on the *Scottish Daily Express* (1963-68)

'This book is a fascinating reminder of Scottish journalism in its heyday. It will be read avidly by those journalists who take pride in their profession – and should be compulsory reading for those who don't.'

JACK WEBSTER, columnist on *The Herald* and *Scottish Daily Express* journalist (1960-80)

The Crofting Years

Francis Thompson

ISBN 0 946487 06 5 PBK £6.95

Crofting is much more than a way of life. It is a storehouse of cultural, linguistic and moral values which holds together a scattered and struggling rural population. This book fills a blank in the written history of crofting over the last two centuries. Bloody conflicts and gunboat diplomacy, treachery, compassion,

music and story: all figure in this mine of information on crofting in the Highlands and Islands of Scotland.

'I would recommend this book to all who are interested in the past, but even more so to those who are interested in the future survival of our way of life and culture'

STORNOWAY GAZETTE

'The book is a mine of information on many aspects of the past, among them the homes, the food, the music and the medicine of our crofting forebears.'

John M Macmillan, erstwhile CROFTERS COMMISSIONER FOR LEWIS AND HARRIS

HISTORY

On the Trail of William Wallace

David R. Ross

ISBN 0 946487 47 2 PBK £7.99

How close to reality was *Braveheart*?

Where was Wallace actually born?

What was the relationship between Wallace and Bruce?

Are there any surviving eye-witness accounts of Wallace?

How does Wallace influence the psyche of today's Scots?

On the Trail of William Wallace offers a refreshing insight into the life and heritage of the great Scots hero whose proud story is at the very heart of what it means to be Scottish. Not concentrating simply on the hard historical facts of Wallace's life, the book also takes into account the real significance of Wallace and his effect on the ordinary Scot through the ages, manifested in the many sites where his memory is marked.

In trying to piece together the jigsaw of the reality of Wallace's life, David Ross weaves a subtle flow of new informa-tion with his own observa-tions. His engaging, thoughtful and at times amusing narrative reads with the ease of a historical novel, complete with all the intrigue, treachery and romance required to hold the attention of the casual reader and still entice the more knowledgable historian.

- 74 places to visit in Scotland and the north of England
- One general map and 3 location maps
- Stirling and Falkirk battle plans
- Wallace's route through London
- Chapter on Wallace connections in North America and elsewhere
- Reproductions of rarely seen illus-trations

On the Trail of William Wallace will be enjoyed by anyone with an interest in Scotland, from the passing tourist to the most fervent nationalist. It is an ency-clopaedia-cum-guide book, literally stuffed with fascinating titbits not usu-ally on offer in the conventional history book.

David Ross is organiser of and historical adviser to the Society of William Wallace.

'Historians seem to think all there is to be known about Wallace has already been uncovered. Mr Ross has proved that Wallace studies are in fact in their infancy.' ELSPETH KING, Director the the Stirling Smith Art Museum & Gallery, who annotated and introduced the recent Luath edition of *Blind Harry's Wallace*.

'Better the pen than the sword!' RANDALL WALLACE, author of *Braveheart,* when asked by David Ross how it felt to be partly responsible for the freedom of a nation following the Devolution Referendum.

POETRY

Blind Harry's Wallace

William Hamilton of Gilbertfield
ISBN 0 946487 43 X HBK £15.00
ISBN 0 946487 33 2 PBK £8.99

The original story of the real braveheart, Sir William Wallace. Racy, blood on every page, violently anglo-phobic, grossly embell-ished, vulgar and dis-gus-ting, clumsy and stilted, a literary failure, a great epic.

Whatever the verdict on BLIND HARRY, this is the book which has done more than any other to frame the notion of Scotland's national identity. Despite its numerous 'historical inaccuracies', it remains the principal source for what we now know about the life of Wallace. The novel and film *Braveheart* were based on the 1722 Hamilton edition of this epic poem. Burns, Wordsworth, Byron and others were greatly influenced by this version 'wherein the old obsolete words are rendered more intelligible', which is said to be the book, next to the Bible, most common-ly found in Scottish households in the eighteenth century. Burns even admits to having 'borrowed... a couplet wor-thy of Homer' directly from Hamilton's version of BLIND HARRY to include in 'Scots wha hae'.

Elspeth King, in her introduction to this, the first accessible edition of BLIND HARRY in verse form since 1859, draws parallels between the situation in Scotland at the time of Wallace and that in Bosnia and Chechnya in the 1990s.

Seven hundred years to the day after the Battle of Stirling Bridge, the 'Settled Will of the Scottish People' was expressed in the devolution referendum of 11 September 1997. She describes this as a landmark opportunity for mature reflection on how the nation has been shaped, and sees BLIND HARRY'S WALLACE as an essential and compelling text for this purpose.

'Builder of the literary foundations of a national hero-cult in a free and powerful country'.

ALEXANDER STODDART, sculptor

'A true bard of the people'.

TOM SCOTT, THE PENGUIN BOOK OF SCOTTISH VERSE, on **Blind Harry.**

'A more inventive writer than Shakespeare'.

RANDALL WALLACE

'The story of Wallace poured a Scottish prejudice in my veins which will boil along until the floodgates of life shut in eternal rest'.

ROBERT BURNS

'Hamilton's couplets are not the best poetry you will ever read, but they rattle along at a fair pace. In re-issuing this work, the publishers have re-opened the spring from which most of our conceptions of the Wallace legend come'.

SCOTLAND ON SUNDAY

'The return of Blind Harry's Wallace, a man who makes Mel look like a wimp'.

THE SCOTSMAN

Poems to be read aloud

Collected and with an introduction by Tom Atkinson

ISBN 0 946487 00 6 PBK £5.00

This personal collection of doggerel and verse ranging from the tear-jerking *Green Eye of the Yellow God* to the rarely printed, bawdy *Eskimo Nell* has a lively cult following. Much borrowed and rarely returned, this is a book for reading aloud in very good company, preferably after a dram or twa. You are guaranteed a warm welcome if you arrive at a gathering with this little volume in your pocket.

'This little book is an attempt to stem the great rushing tide of canned entertainment. A hopeless attempt of course. There is poetry of very high order here, but there is also some fearful doggerel. But that is the way of things. No literary axe is being ground. Of course some of the items in this book are poetic drivel, if read as poems. But that is not the point. They all spring to life when they are read aloud. It is the combination of the poem with your voice, with all the art and craft you can muster, that produces the finished product and effect you seek. You don't have to learn the poems. Why clutter up your mind with rubbish? Of course, it is a poorly furnished mind that doesn't carry a fair stock of poetry, but surely the poems to be remembered and savoured in secret, when in love, or ill, or sad, are not the ones you want to share with an audience. So go ahead, clear your throat and transfix all talkers with a stern eye, then let rip!'

TOM ATKINSON

Luath Press Limited
committed to publishing well written books worth reading

LUATH PRESS takes its name from Robert Burns, whose little collie Luath (*Gael.,* swift or nimble) tripped up Jean Armour at a wedding and gave him the chance to speak to the woman who was to be his wife and the abiding love of his life. Burns called one of *The Twa Dogs* Luath after Cuchullin's hunting dog in *Ossian's Fingal.* Luath Press grew up in the heart of Burns country, and now resides a few steps up the road from Burns' first lodgings in Edinburgh's Royal Mile.

Luath offers you distinctive writing with a hint of unexpected pleasures.

Most UK bookshops either carry our books in stock or can order them for you. To order direct from us, please send a £sterling cheque, postal order, international money order or your credit card details (number, address of cardholder and expiry date) to us at the address below. Please add post and packing as follows: UK – £1.00 per delivery address; overseas surface mail – £2.50 per delivery address; overseas airmail – £3.50 for the first book to each delivery address, plus £1.00 for each additional book by airmail to the same address. If your order is a gift, we will happily enclose your card or message at no extra charge.

Luath Press Limited
543/2 Castlehill
The Royal Mile
Edinburgh EH1 2ND
Telephone: 0131 225 4326 (24 hours)
Fax: 0131 225 4324
email: gavin.macdougall@luath.co.uk
Website: www.luath.co.uk